Transforming Learning

Introducing SEAL Approaches

Compiled by

Susan Norman

Published by Saffire Press for SEAL (Society for Effective Affective Learning)

First published October 2003

Published by

Saffire Press
37 Park Hall Road
East Finchley
London N2 9PT, UK

Fax +44(0)20 8444 0339
Email seal@saffirepress.co.uk
www.saffirepress.co.uk

The book is published on behalf of

SEAL (Society for Effective Affective Learning)
37 Park Hall Road
East Finchley
London N2 9PT, UK

Fax +44(0)20 8444 0339
Email seal@seal.org.uk
www.seal.org.uk

Layout and design by Susan Norman and Hugh L'Estrange

Printed in Great Britain by Ashford Colour Press, Gosport, Hants PO13 0FW

ISBN 1 901564 06 1

Foreword

by

Sir Christopher Ball

Patron of SEAL

Chancellor of the University of Derby
Founder of the National Campaign for Learning
Chairman of The Talent Foundation

Here is a treasure chest. Dip into it – and I defy you not to find something of value for yourself. I love the delightful mindmaps, apposite quotations and annotated book lists. Reading it in draft, I was reminded of the transformational work of Vygotsky, Gardner and Goleman, moved again by the inspiration of NVC, Reggio Emilia and music, and gently introduced to treasures I have yet to sample, like NLP, PhotoReading and meditation.

People learn best in an environment of high challenge and low stress. This book offers just such an experience. There is a lot to learn, if you want to – and nothing to fear. I find the emphasis on the spiritual dimension rather challenging, since I don't think I have one! (Blind spot or insight?) Others will find other challenges. That is OK. There are no brownie points for learning what we already know – and few for learning only what we know we don't know. The aim of transformational learning is to help us learn what we don't know we don't know.

I am proud to be the patron of SEAL. It is a society that I could not afford not to be a member of, since its publications, conferences and members repeatedly take me to the leading edge of learning. The membership of SEAL is broad and diverse, their interests are likewise wide-ranging and varied, but they have in common three key characteristics or passions – body, brain and heart. SEAL's holistic approach to learning unites physical experience with mental discipline and emotional integrity. If we ever develop a true science of learning, as I hope we shall, it must respect each of these aspects of being.

People often ask me what SEAL is about. Read this book and find out.

Those who love wisdom must investigate many things

HERACLITUS

SEAL

Society for Effective Affective Learning

SEAL was founded in 1983 at a conference of IATEFL (International Association for English as a Foreign Language) by Peter O'Connell (1918-1998) and Michael Lawlor (1930-1997) to promote suggestopedia, the work of Georgi Lozanov. Most of the concepts covered in this book have been presented at SEAL conferences which are renowned for their exploration of the leading edge of learning,

SEAL's membership has grown over the years. Members are typically teachers, trainers and counsellors – language teachers, teachers and lecturers in all fields and educational institutions, business trainers, personal development counsellors and therapists. We are also proud to count a few sports coaches, doctors and scientists among our members. Many of them are working at the leading edge in their own fields and want to engage with the wide variety of disciplines you'll find represented here. Many of the recommended books have been written by SEAL members.

> *Affect –*
> *to do with the*
> *emotions,*
> *as in the word*
> *'affection'*

The importance of SEAL is the way it crosses the usual boundaries and brings together people from very different fields who wouldn't normally meet, but when you look at the many different 'approaches', you find much common ground. For over 20 years, SEAL has been providing the opportunity for this cross-fertilisation of ideas that leads to such a unique and exciting synergism.

'The leading edge of learning' can sometimes be an uncomfortable and lonely place – as most people working there will attest. A great benefit of belonging to SEAL is the relief of being with like-minded people who share your passion for learning.

SEAL has sometimes been accused of being like a jolly party on board ship, sailing off over the horizon, but having little impact on those behind who can't tell from the wake what all the fuss is about. This book then is the pleasure steamer. It gives an introduction to many of the ideas that are espoused by SEAL members. It is a starting point for anyone interested in sorting out the difference between Multiple Intelligence theory and learning styles, or NLP and AL, and a host of other things. This is what all the fuss is about!

It is really exciting to notice the recent interest in brain-friendly approaches and ideas from Accelerated Learning beginning to make headway in mainstream education. They are also gaining credibility in companies, who recognise their worth – and their impact on the bottom line! The time is right for these ideas to come into their own.

There are thriving communities in many countries which share SEAL's mission to promote holistic approaches to learning. Some consist of groups of SEAL members (in Argentina, The Netherlands, Israel and elsewhere), others are associate organisations in their own right, the two largest being IAL (International Alliance for Learning, www.ialearn.org) in the US and DGSL (Deutsche Gesellschaft für suggestopädagogisches Lehren und Lernen, www.dgsl.de) in Germany.

Why not be part of this international learning community?
Join SEAL
It's where you belong!

Introduction

This book is an attempt to answer the question
'What is SEAL about?'
It is aimed primarily at teachers, trainers and anybody who is passionate about learning.
It is a starting point for anyone setting out
on their journey of personal and professional discovery.
It defines concepts,
makes practical teaching suggestions where appropriate,
and gives an annotated booklist and sources of further information.
You are invited to investigate and incorporate
those things which seem to make sense to you,
which fit with your values and skills,
and which seem most likely to benefit the students you teach.
There is not one SEAL Approach.
SEAL promotes all holistic approaches and methods,
those which take account of the whole person:

Body
Movement enhances learning.

Emotions
Emotional competence can release many of the blocks to learning.

Mind
The mind is essential to learning, but it cannot work effectively
unless bodily and emotional needs are taken care of.

Spirit
Human beings also have a spiritual dimension
which needs to be acknowledged.

Relationships
People do not exist in a vacuum.
Any approach which takes account of the individuality of the learner
also needs to take account of that learner in relationship to others.

Many of these approaches have been around for a long time.
Some you will be familiar with, some may be new.
They are all different slants on a central message which is that:
every person is a unique individual with a unique approach to learning.
This individuality needs to be addressed in any teaching situation.
If you teach the learner in the way most appropriate to them,
then the content will take care of itself.
We are concerned first with the 'who' and the 'how' of learning.
The 'what' follows naturally.

Acknowledgements

One of the best things about working for SEAL is learning about the vast range of ideas which have been presented at SEAL Conferences and which are the stuff of life of our many members throughout the world. This book is an attempt to bring together as many of those ideas as possible. In undertaking this task, I happily acknowledge the huge debt I owe to SEAL, to many SEAL members and presenters at SEAL Conferences whose sessions I have been privileged to attend and whose books and articles I have read. There are too many to mention here by name, although many of them feature within the text, but I offer huge thanks to all the passionate and inspiring people who make SEAL the wonderful organisation it is.

In particular, though, I would like to thank the people who have contributed directly to this publication: Sir Christopher Ball, SEAL's patron since 1999, for his generous foreword and personal support; Rita Baker, Richard Barrett, Robin Cain, Jan Cisek, Howard Gardner, Eva Hoffman, Grethe Hooper Hansen, Julie Hay, Shirley Laflin, Mark McKergow, Katrina Patterson, Anne-Mijke van Harten for their contributions of articles and ideas; Jill Johnson for much of the original structure; Hilarie Bowman for her suggestion at a Welwyn & Hatfield SEAL meeting that we should produce 'something like an A-Z of SEAL Approaches'. This is not quite an A-Z … but I hope it's a start.

Whatever failings the book may have are down to me. I would welcome comments and suggestions for improvements in a future edition.

Thanks are due too to all the people who have supported the publication of this book financially: all those who have taken advertisements at the end of the book, and especially Bob Beale and Diane Dávalos-Beale (a most gifted suggestopedic teacher – check out www.expanded-learning.com) for their very generous donation.

My biggest thanks go to Hugh L'Estrange, Co-Director of SEAL, for his editorial contributions, and most of all for the joy of sharing the exploration.

Susan Norman
Co-Director of SEAL

Contents

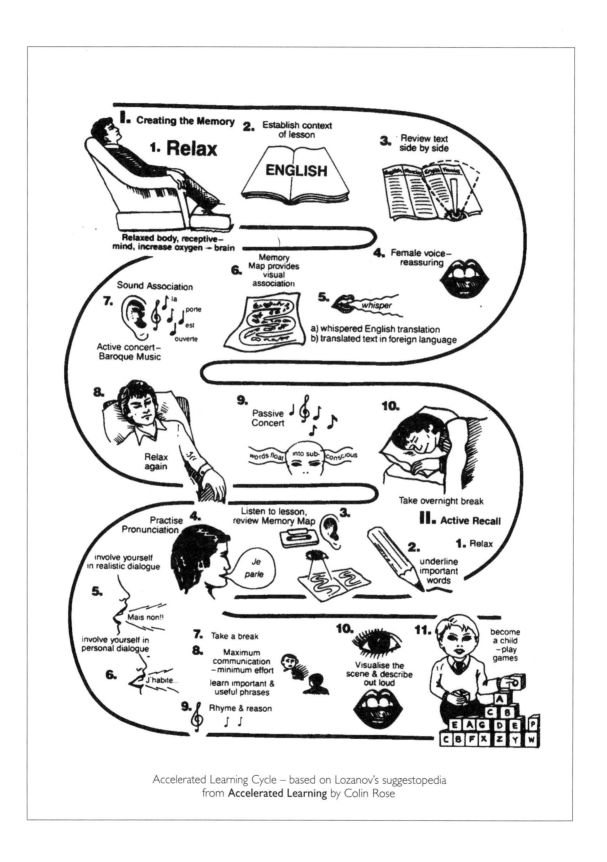

Accelerated Learning Cycle – based on Lozanov's suggestopedia
from **Accelerated Learning** by Colin Rose

Accelerated Learning

Accelerated Learning has become something of a catch-all phrase, largely synonymous with brain-based or mind-friendly learning. It is derived from Lozanov's suggestopedia (page 45). Lozanov began his research in Bulgaria in the 1960s, and during the 70s he trained a small number of people in the US in his methods. In 1980 he was placed under house arrest in Bulgaria, and for the next 10 years was not allowed to communicate with the outside world. During this time, his trainees in the US continued to teach and develop what was now being called 'Accelerated Learning' or 'Accelerative Learning', each adhering to the basic principles, but with differing practices.

AL can be interpreted at three levels:

1 **Basic AL** The tools and techniques of Accelerated Learning are used to augment and enhance traditional curriculum and teaching methods.
2 **Full AL** The whole programme of classroom management, the curriculum and teaching methods are designed to be congruent with brain function and learning styles.
3 **Transformational AL** At a transformative level, there is an awareness of the personal development of the students which is achieved through the learning process. Teachers also know that their ability to teach others well depends on their own understanding of themselves, so good teachers are continually working on their own personal and professional growth.

At all levels of AL, though, it is important to remember that the substance and content is every bit as important as the 'sizzle'. Many people pick up on the fun aspect of AL, which is important, but it is important in the context of on-going learning, not as an end in itself.

The first part of this book expands and explains what is involved in an Accelerated Learning approach to teaching and learning.

....

WHAT DOES AL CONSIST OF?

Some AL courses conform very much to the suggestopedic model (page 45), but the things which would be important in any AL course are the following. Those things which are not self-evident are treated separately in other sections of the book.

- Knowledge about the human brain and learning (page 14)
- Understanding how emotion affects learning (pages 16, 32, 37)
- The importance of the learning environment (page 41)
- The importance of movement (page 20)
- The role of music (page 42) and the arts
- Giving an overview
- Setting clear goals
- Giving much more new information than in a 'normal' session

- Multiple Intelligence theory (page 29)
- Learning styles (page 33)
- The power of story, metaphor, imagination and visualisation (page 26)
- Suggestion – to create a positive mental state
- The importance of self-esteem (page 40)
- Personal motivation
- Teaching to the non-conscious mind (page 22)
- Team learning and co-operation
- Review
- Improvement and quantifiable results
- Celebration

GETTING STARTED

A practical approach for getting started is the 'Quantum Learning' model, developed by Bobbi DePorter, who runs 'SuperCamp' – fun summer schools in the US. (Other models are very similar.) The lesson sequence runs like this (with example activities in italics):

ENROL Hook the students with an intriguing opening statement and global picture of the lesson. Arouse their curiosity. Give them a glimpse of what is to come without revealing too much. • *Draw a picture on the board – students guess what it represents.* • *Make up an advertising-type slogan about why the lesson's going to be important/fun/interesting.* • *Ask challenging questions, eg 'If you suddenly found yourself in an isolated area of the Sierra in the US mountains, how would you survive?'*

EXPERIENCE Give students an experience or activity that demonstrates the lesson. Create a need to know. An experience creates curiosity and emotional engagement. It allows students to tap into prior knowledge and make connections, adding meaning and relevance to the content. • *Several students act out (under your direction) the way information travels in bits and bytes from one computer to another.* • *All students working in groups put information cards in sequence/date order.* • *Give an overview of the conditions they'll endure in the Sierra mountains – they work in groups to plan what they might do in response to anticipated challenges.*

LABEL Give the 'data' at the moment of peak interest and discuss its relevance to students' lives. Explaining the lesson after the experience capitalises on the students' natural desire to label, sequence and define new learning. • *Give out a written summary of the information (or direct students to the coursebook) – and ask them to do something, eg identify the one bit of information that you haven't yet covered, or check their own sequencing of information cards.* • *Read aloud a relevant story, eg about the early settlers in the US.*

DEMONSTRATE Provide opportunities for students to translate and apply their new knowledge to other situations. Giving students additional activities demonstrates to them what they know and builds confidence. • *Students write a section of a computer instruction manual.* • *Teacher reads out a sequence and students spot deliberate errors.* • *In groups, students show still snapshots related to the story, eg of settler family members in the middle of a dramatic moment in their lives – others guess who they represent and what's going on.*

REVIEW Quickly summarise what the lesson has been about. Review strengthens the brain's neural connections, increasing retention. • *In groups, students make up a jingle to summarise their main learning in the lesson.* • *Students turn to a neighbour and say one thing they learnt or enjoyed.* • *Everyone stands up and shouts out at the same time something they've learnt.*

CELEBRATE Celebrate the students' success. Celebration honours effort, diligence and success. Anything from high fives or clapping, to smiles or a quiet word of congratulation from the teacher, or from student to student.

If I had only to pick one thing to focus on as a starting point for AL, it would definitely be the relationship between teacher and students. A teacher who is approachable, who listens, who supports and helps students, who likes and respects students, who talks pleasantly to students – such a teacher is already doing Accelerated Learning.

> *Children don't care how much you know until they know how much you care*

Brain-Based Learning

Accelerated Learning is based on what we now understand about the brain and how we learn. Here then is a summary by one of the masters of these things which are considered 'brain-based' or 'brain-friendly'.

Not brain-compatible	YES: Brain-Based
Low emotional impact	Appropriately high emotional arousal
Fragmented, sequential only	Global, unified, thematic, real life
Standard boring illustrations	Colourful, abundant memory maps
Suppressing learner energy	Utilizing and expressing energy
Lecture, more didactic	Multiple intelligences served
Emphasis on content	Emphasis on context, meaning and value
Resigned to the learner's state	Positively conditions the learner and states
Mistakes recognized directly	Mistakes noted indirectly or reframed
Learner association with failure	Use of alter-ego, other fun characters
Subjects taught separately	Cross-curricular learning
Emphasis on quiet learning	Often rich with talking, music, activity
Belief that learning is difficult	Attitude is: it's easy, fun and creative
Creates tension and stress to learn	Keeps stress low and enjoyment high
Learning as only mental/cognitive	Learning also as action, movement
Quest for a single answer	Search for questions
Forced learning driven by grades	Intrinsic motivation evoked with need
Central focused stimuli	Use of significant peripheral stimuli
Extended presenter lecture time	Alternate focus and diffusion activities
Assumes authority from role	Creates constant respect and credibility
Finish when time's up	Finish with celebration
Subtle or obvious threats, helplessness	Remove threats; focus on support
Focus on learning in classrooms	Real world, simulations, trips
Institutional boring rituals	Positive, purposeful rituals
Infer, tell, demand	Suggest, ask, tell
Insistent focus on conscious learning	Use of strong non-conscious learning
Minimal open and closing time	Longer open and close, shorter middle
Delayed, indefinite vague feedback	Immediate dramatic feedback
Teach for the test, with stress	Learn for the joy of learning and real life
Sit at desks and limit interactions	Mobility, face each other, partners, groups
Abrupt exposure to content	Purposeful and consistent pre-exposure
Introduce topic, forget it	Multiple exposure and activation at 1-3 days
Outcome-based mandated learning	Our best learning is **not** measurable
Constant use of negations; many 'don'ts'	Use of totally positive language
Use of bribes, rewards, gimmicks	Intrinsic motivation elicited
Starve the brain of stimulation	Enriched; music, sights, aromas, movement
Disciplined, ordered, quiet, repressive	Expressive, changing, noisy, music
Single topic only by presenter choice	Learner input on topics

From **Brain-Based Learning** by Eric Jensen

From **For You, Dear Teacher** by Eva Hoffman; artwork Justina Langley

---

ON-GOING QUESTIONS

- Are excellent teachers born or made? Is AL a series of techniques, skills, attitudes and behaviours which can be learnt, and which, if learnt, lead to inspirational teaching? Is it the AL method which makes a teacher excellent, or is any excellent teacher, by definition, an AL teacher?

- What is learning? Is it something you do or something that happens – possibly as a result of something you do?

- How do you know when you know something? How do you measure 'soft' outcomes?

MORE TO EXPLORE

ABOUT AL

Colin ROSE **Accelerated Learning** Accelerated Learning Systems Ltd 1985. *Still the best place to start – a very readable introduction.*

Bobbi DePORTER **Quantum Learning** Piatkus 1992. *Describes the 'supercamp' model of AL.*

Gail HEIDENHAIN (ed) **Learning Beyond Boundaries** International Alliance for Learning (IAL) 2003. *Essays from field leaders on aspects and practical implications of AL.*

Gordon DRYDEN & Jeannette VOS **The Learning Revolution** Network Educational Press 2001. *Excellent theory in practice.*

Eric JENSEN **Super Teaching** Brain Store Inc 1995 and **Brain-Based Learning** Turning Point Publishing 1996. *Jensen's many books all focus on linking brain research and practical learning and teaching. (All Jensen's books are worth looking at.)*

Colin ROSE **Master it Faster** Accelerated Learning Systems Ltd 1999. *Introduction to AL aimed at learners. Also now available on CD-ROM.*

Bill LUCAS **Power Up Your Mind – learn faster, work smarter** Nicholas Brealey 2001. *Good practical starting point.*

AL IN SCHOOLS

Alistair SMITH, Nicola CALL **The ALPS Approach** Network Educational Press 1999. *Implementing a complete AL approach in primary schools.*

Mark FLETCHER **Teaching for Success – the brain-friendly revolution in action** Brain Friendly Publications 2000. *Practical AL teaching ideas.*

Paul GINNIS **The Teacher's Toolkit – raise classroom acheivement with strategies for every learner** Crown House Publishing 2002. *Written by a practising secondary teacher – very usable.*

Diane LOOMANS, Karen KOLBERG **The Laughing Classroom** H J Kramer Books & New World Library 1993. *Lots of lovely ideas for making lessons more fun.*

JOB **The Great Little Book of Brainpower** (2001) and **The Great Little Book of Revision** (2002) The Quantum Group. *Fun little books, popular with teenagers.*

AL IN BUSINESS

Dave MEIER **The Accelerated Learning Handbook** McGraw-Hill 2000. *Practical AL slanted towards business.*

Colin ROSE **AL System 2000** – *4 books, 3 videos and 3 audio cassettes, now available only from SEAL.*

Kimberley HARE, Larry REYNOLDS **51 Tools for Transforming Training** Gower 2002. *Practical application of AL to business. (Paperback version available 2004)*

MORE RECOMMENDATIONS FOR BUSINESS

Big Book of Business Games series McGraw-Hill: **Team-Building, Humorous Training, Presentation, Business, Creativity, Customer Service, Sales, Stress Relief.** *Good source of business training activities. See also* **Games Trainers Play series** McGraw Hill.

Mark Victor HANSEN, Robert ALLEN **The One Minute Millionaire** Vermillion 2002. *A novel about how one woman transformed her working life, and on alternate pages the methods and principles by which she does it.*

See also bibliography for **Suggestopedia** (page 47)

· ·

MIND MAPPING

Tony Buzan invented Mind Mapping® – a system for recording information in a way which is more compatible with the way the brain works than linear text. Start with your central concept and draw lines radiating out from it, writing one word to represent each connected main idea. Smaller branches radiate out from the main branches with subsidiary ideas and examples. Use colours, pictures and lines to link related ideas on different branches. Mind map to take notes from books or talks and to make your own plans for a talk or for written reports, essays, articles, etc. Each mind map will be unique, and easier to remember because of its visual impact, and each can be added to – it grows organically, which is how we think. You'll find examples on pages 30 and 41.

VISUAL LANGUAGE

Mind mapping is one example of visual language – the combination of pictures, diagrams, symbols and words which we are most familiar with in advertising and road signs, but which is likely to become more and more prevalent as the quickest and most effective way of presenting information.

A picure's worth a thousand words.

MORE TO EXPLORE

Tony BUZAN, Barry BUZAN **The Mind Map Book – how to use radiant thinking to maximize your brain's untapped potential** Plume 1996. *The original book.*

Eva HOFFMAN **Introducing Children to Mind Mapping** Learn to Learn 2001

Nancy MARGULIES **Mapping Inner Space – learning and teaching visual mapping** Zephyr Press 2001

Robert HORN **Visual Language** Macro Vu Press

The Brain

How does the brain work? It depends who you're asking. A neuroscientist? A biologist? A geneticist? A psychiatrist? Basically we still have more questions than answers. More is being learnt about how the brain works every day and more has been learnt in the last 25 years than was ever known before, so the important thing is to keep up to date. The brain is not just a physical entity. Gone are the days when specific areas of the brain were deemed responsible for specific parts of the body, emotions or thoughts. If one part of the brain is damaged, it is often possible for other parts to take over the function/s it was performing. Much of what was believed in the past has been disproved. Much more has been proved to be only part of the picture. And even when the scientists 'know' and can prove certain things about the brain, there is still a big jump from that to deciding how that affects learning and teaching.

Although the ideas presented here are oversimplifications, the basic implications for learning are valid. There are 100 billion neurons in our brain which are constantly reaching out to one another. If an electrical impulse of information crosses the synaptic gap between one neuron and another, a learning pathway is created. The more the pathway is used, the stronger it gets – learning is consolidated. The more pathways we have connecting a piece of information to other things we know, the more ways we have of remembering and retrieving it we have. One piece of good news: apparently the brain does go on producing new cells right up to the day we die – it's not just a case of making new connections. But the message is still the same: use it or lose it. Actively using your brain is the best way to keep it working for you.

Most of the influences on the brain – and therefore on thinking – are physical and chemical, so food, the environment, breathing and movement have a crucial effect on the brain, on our emotions, and on our ability to learn.

BASIC REST AND ACTIVITY CYCLE (BRAC)

BRAC is the body's fundamental 90-120 minute cycle of rest and activity originally discovered by Eugene Aserinsky and Nathaniel Kleitman in 1953. In practice this means that the optimum cycle is to work for about 90 minutes and then take a 20-minute rest with a longer break in the middle of the day. The rest phases, both during the day and at night, when it occurs as REM (rapid eye movement) sleep, is important for long-term memory and learning at a cellular level, when genes are literally 'turned on' (known as 'gene expression'). There are other cycles too which mean that we need approximately eight hours sleep in a day, and that we need to take holidays occasionally to completely switch off from work.

Rest periods are essential to our continuing health and creativity. We can force ourselves to break these pattern and work much longer hours, but in the long-run it leads to the build-up of stress and ill-health – and even in the short term, we are working much less effectively.

Thanks to Katrina Patterson for this information.

E ROSSI and D CHEEK **The Psychobiology of Mind-Body Healing** (Revised ed) 1993. *Scientific explanations for the body's natural rhythms.*

E ROSSI **The Psychobiology of Gene Expression: Neuroscience, Neurogenesis and Numinosum in Psychotherapy and the Healing Arts** Norton 2002. *The latest information about gene changes during sleep.*

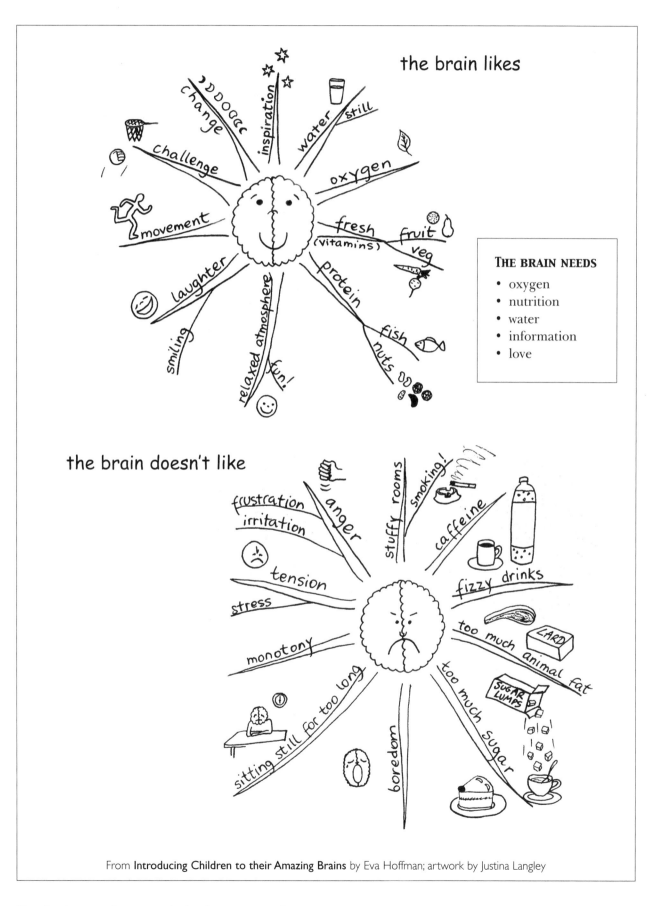

the brain likes

THE BRAIN NEEDS
- oxygen
- nutrition
- water
- information
- love

the brain doesn't like

From **Introducing Children to their Amazing Brains** by Eva Hoffman; artwork by Justina Langley

THE TRIUNE BRAIN

Paul MacLean's theory (1967) was that the structure of the brain reflects its evolution, and that there are three basic parts. The **reptilian brain** is centered on the brain stem and mainly controls the body's basic survival systems: breathing, heart rate, movement, temperature, etc. The key motivator is *'survival/avoiding harm'*. The central area of the brain is the **limbic system**, the 'mammalian brain', which is responsible for the emotions and plays an important part in long-term memory. Its key motivator is *'hunt for pleasure'*. Higher thinking (planning, abstract thought) is centred in the **neo-cortex**, the wrinkled part you see covering the outside of the brain which is separated into the two hemispheres. The key motivator is *'quest for novelty'*.

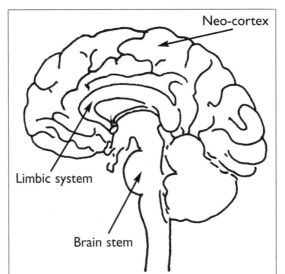

Apparently neuroscientists no longer find the concept of the 'triune brain' useful, but since it ties in with Maslow's hierarchy of needs (below) and emotional intelligence (page 32), it can still be of interest to educators.

The **Reticular Activating System (RAS)** in the upper brain stem controls which part of the brain is in charge. People's first need is to have their physical requirements met. You cannot learn if you are in physical danger, need to go to the toilet, are hungry, or too hot or too cold. Nor can you learn if you are in an overly emotional or stressed state. While emotional attachment aids memory, strong emotions unconnected with the learning experience, whether positive or negative, interfere with learning.

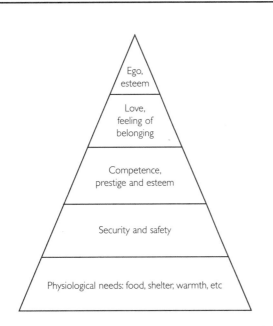

ABRAHAM MASLOW'S 'HIERARCHY OF NEEDS'

Maslow's triangle shows how people are motivated. The needs at the base of the triangle must be satisfied before those higher up come into play.

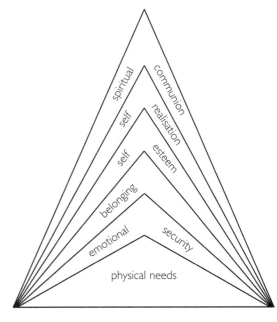

Hava Jonai's adaptation of Maslow's triangle shows that all aspects of the personality are present at all times, albeit in different proportions. It also adds a sixth element: spiritual communion.

RIGHT-LEFT BRAIN

Assign these different attributes to the left or right hemisphere of the neo-cortex. (Answers next page)

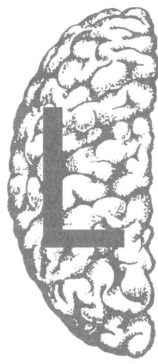

ANALYSIS	ORGANISED
CAUSE & EFFECT	PART TO WHOLE
CONNECTING	PATTERN
CONTROLLED	POSSIBILITY
DISCRETE ITEMS	RELAXED
DISORGANISED	RHYTHM
EXPERIMENTAL	SEQUENCE
FACT	SPONTANEITY
HIGHER MATHS	STRUCTURE
IMAGINATION	SUBJECTIVE
INTUITIVE	SYNTHESIS
LANGUAGE	THEORETICAL
LOGIC	TUNE
MEASURING	WHAT IF ...
NUMBER	WHAT IS ...
OBJECTIVE	WHOLE THEN DETAIL

Ready to further learning aims and objectives

Increasing sense of autonomy in learning

Self-esteem enhanced by success in realising learning objectives; sense of identity within group

Team building; attention to individual learning styles and development needs; friendly supportive environment

Zero stress; no fear of failure – removal of learning blocks; well-structured environment, efficient organisation

All basic physical needs catered for

Maslow's triangle adapted for learning by Rita Baker, again showing a sixth level.

MORE TO EXPLORE

Alistair SMITH **The Brain's Behind It** Network Educational Press 2002. *Practical, well-researched summary shedding a sensible light on some of the myths and exaggerations which result from science being popularised. Best read.*

Peter RUSSELL **The Brain Book** Routledge & Kegan Paul 1979. *Even though written so long ago, it still has much to say of relevance to educators.*

Rita CARTER **Mapping the Mind** Weidenfeld & Nicolson 1998. *Most comprehensive and readable introduction to the mind/brain.*

Rita CARTER **Exploring Consciousness** University of California Press 2002. *Similarly exciting read about the nature of the mind and consciousness.*

John McCRONE **How the Brain Works – a beginner's guide to the mind and consciousness** Dorling Kindersley 2002. *A quick (cheap) whistle-stop overview.*

Susan GREENFIELD **Brainpower – working out the human mind** Element Books 1999. *Accessible well-illustrated popular overview.*

Eva HOFFMAN **Introducing Children to their Amazing Brains** Learn to Learn 2002. *Well-illustrated photocopiable resource making brain information accessible to children. Particularly useful for the 36 brain questions and answers.*

RIGHT-LEFT BRAIN

Roger Sperry won the Nobel prize in medicine in 1981 for 'discoveries concerning the functional specialization of the cerebral hemispheres'. Since then the media and others have leapt onto the bandwagon of allocating different functions to the right and left hemisphere. In simplistic terms the right takes a global view and the left deals with details. However as soon as you start allocating abilities to one or other side, you need to be very specific – well beyond what is necessary for teaching purposes. There are areas relating to language, for example, situated in various parts of the brain. These are mostly on the left, while the right processes linguistic context. While music appreciation seems to be located mainly on the right, musicians who are learning and studying music, or those who are listening critically to specific aspects of the music, will also be using significant areas of the left hemisphere. Then again, if parts of the brain are damaged, certain functions that have been lost can sometimes be transferred to different parts of the brain and gradually be regained.

Learning – or doing anything – always involves activity in both hemispheres, and the important thing is the transfer of information between the hemispheres through the corpus callosum. All learners learn better when both sides of the brain are involved in the learning process.

In reality, school and most formal teaching situations are geared towards the traditional concept of the logical 'left-brained learner' and it is the so-called right-brained learners (those who don't follow the step-by-step logic easily and need a big picture and seem to make intuitive leaps of understanding) who are often failed by the system. Teachers, almost by definition, are those who have flourished in the system, and it is not always easy for us to understand that there are people who need to learn in different ways. Therefore, if the concept of the R/L brain gives us a justification for taking a significantly different approach to teaching for at least 50% of the time, then it is a useful concept. The important thing is to teach to all types of learner.

Appropriate 'brain-friendly' techniques and activities for teaching creativity will make it easier for 'right-brained learners' to learn – and will enhance the learning process for all learners.

> *'The more we learn, the more we recognize the unique complexity of any one individual intellect, the stronger the conclusion becomes that the individuality inherent in our brain networks makes that of fingerprints or facial features gross and simple by comparison.'*
>
> ROGER SPERRY
>
> (NOBEL PRIZE ACCEPTANCE SPEECH, 1981)

ANSWERS TO R/L BRAIN PUZZLE (PREVIOUS PAGE)

Although these answers are oversimplifications and both hemispheres are involved in most types of thinking, in broad terms it can be useful to differentiate between left-brain and right-brain thinking.

RIGHT Connecting • Disorganised • Experimental • Higher maths • Imagination • Intuitive • Pattern • Possibility • Relaxed • Rhythm • Spontaneity • Subjective • Synthesis • Tune • What if … • Whole then detail

LEFT Analysis • Cause & effect • Controlled • Discrete items • Fact • Language • Logic • Measuring • Number • Objective • Organised • Part to whole • Sequence • Structure • Theoretical • What is …

Brain-body dominances

Most people are 'wired' so that one side of their brain is dominant. Have a look at the typical characteristics of each side of the brain on the opposite page. Which one best describes you? Nor is it just brain hemisphere dominance which affects how you operate effectively. Are you right or left handed? You almost certainly know. But do you also know your dominant eye, foot and ear? They can make a significant difference to the way you learn. Western society is set up more for right-handed (and left-brained) people, but did you also know that it is easier to read European script (from left to right) if you have a dominant right eye – and if the left hemisphere is dominant you will find it easier to understand what you read. Having the opposite dominance does not necessarily mean that you will have learning difficulties, but people with learning difficulties often have that dominance. Footballers know whether they have a dominant right or left foot, but just as most players of sport can have a significant advantage if they are equally proficient with both hands and both feet, so everyone can operate more effectively if they develop both sides of their body optimally.

Knowing your dominant eye, ear, brain, hand and foot can improve your learning

GESTALT DOMINANT
FULL SENSORY ACCESS

(dominant right brain, left eye, ear, hand and foot)

- Learns best through movement and by focusing on whole picture, context and emotional relevance to self.
- Must be able to see, hear, move and/or verbalize whole context before learning details.
- Appreciates metaphors, examples and associations when problem solving. Looks and listens for the intention and emotion of the person and/or information.
- Interprets language primarily from its tone, pitch and rhythm (dialect).
- Learns kinesthetically, needing to move (especially the hands) to process new learning. Physically and emotionally expressive.
- Quickly grasps the main idea but may have great difficulty seeing, hearing and communicating the details in a linear way.
- Is often highly intuitive and prefers to process that way.
- Left eye scans from right to left. Possible difficulty reading or writing languages that move from left to right like English. May reverse or transpose letters and/or numbers.
- Has difficulty following step-by-step instructions. Tends to start by imagining the end results and then intuitively doing what seems appropriate.
- Movements tend to be spontaneous and fluid – freeform – but the capacity to exhibit good technique (like a specific dance step) may deteriorate under stress.
- May have difficulty with penmanship. Benefits from fine-motor, hand-eye coordination play and work.
- Because the dominant hand, ear, eye and foot are all opposite the gestalt hemisphere, this learner has no access to the logic hemisphere during new learning or when stressed. This learner's biggest challenge will be to access the pieces of information, be able to put them together in a linear, logical manner and communicate it.

HELPS

- Encouragement and good modeling on how to work and communicate details and linear aspects of life and learning is very important.
- This learner will benefit from sitting toward the front but where they can move without disturbing others.
- Activities that help: integrated cross-lateral movements such as Lazy 8s, Cross-Crawl and Hook Ups from Brain Gym (page 20).
- An integrative balance of art, music, movement and inter/intrapersonal skills combined with cognitive endeavors in linguistics and mathematics will be highly beneficial.

From **The Dominance Factor** by Carla Hannaford

Brain Gym®

The reason why animals have brains and plants don't is because animals move from one place to another. Movement is an essential part of being an animal and it is essential to the growing of new brain cells and connections, and, according to Carla Hannaford (author of *Smart Moves*), it is essential to learning. Brain Gym⁆ or Educational Kinesiology (Edu-K) as it is also known, is a series of simple movements developed by Paul Dennison and Gail Dennison which encourage the brain-body development by stimulating different muscles and parts of the brain and endocrine system. Although any exercise and stretching has positive benefits, Brain Gym is more than this. There are three 'dimensions' (types of exercise), the Laterality Dimension, the Focusing Dimension and the Centering Dimension, whose purposes are to stimulate, release and relax respectively.

EXERCISES TO HELP FOCUS THE EYES, AID CONCENTRATION AND PREPARE FOR READING

LAZY 8S

Hold one arm straight out in front of you with your hand in a fist, thumb pointing up. Starting at the midpoint, moving upwards from your starting point, make a figure of eight horizontally in front of you by circling your hand round to the left anti-clockwise, completing the circle back at the centre and continuing smoothly up and round to the right clockwise, coming back up to the centre again – and keep going. Follow your thumb with your eyes keeping your neck relaxed. Your head may move slightly. Do this three times. Repeat with the other hand, making sure that you are always moving upwards from the middle. Then repeat with both hands clasped together.

DOUBLE DOODLES

Hold both arms out in front of you. Write your name in the air with your normal writing hand, and at the same time mirror-write your name with the other hand, moving in the opposite direction. Right handers start from the centre and move towards the outside; left-handers start at the outside and move towards the centre. Write other words and draw different shapes too.

DOUBLE DOODLES

Illustration from **Brain Gym** by Paul and Gail Dennison

Brain Gym® is a Registered Trademark of the Educational Kinesiology Foundation, Ventura Harbor Village.1575 Spinaker Drive, Suite 204B, Ventura, California CA 930011, USA.

P–A–C–E

PACE, one of the better-known starting points, stands for (in reverse order):

Energy Sipping water regularly keeps body and mind energised.

Clear Massaging the 'brain buttons' (in the hollows just below the clavicles on either side of the breastbone) clears the head. The other hand is placed on the navel.

Active Physical movements where arms and legs cross the mid-line of the body encourage both sides of the brain to work together. Try doing 'cross-crawl': alternately touching one hand (or elbow) to the opposite knee (or ankle). It should be done slowly.

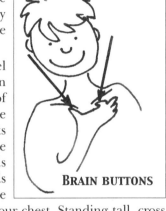

BRAIN BUTTONS

Positive 'Hook ups' help you feel focused and calm. Put both arms out in front of you, thumbs down, backs of hands together. Put one hand over the other so palms are together and wrists are crossed. Clasp the fingers of the hands together. Turn the hands downwards as you move them towards you, bringing them up through the space between your arms to rest on your chest. Standing tall, cross one leg over the other. Keep both feet on the floor. Put your tongue on the roof of your mouth. Breathe deeply and regularly. Hook ups can also be done sitting down.

HOOK-UPS

Illustrations by Justina Langley from **The Learning Adventure** by Eva Hoffman

---

FURTHER DEVELOPMENTS

Further developments to look out for (nothing has yet been published) are:

VISION-GYM Paul and Gail Dennison, the originators of Brain Gym, developed a further 35 movements that release eye tension and integrate visual perception (a key component in whole-brain integration) and hand-eye co-ordination. One result is better vision and improved reading comprehension and retention of information.

VISION CIRCLES The completion of developmental skills through movement, play, art and vision awareness. The eight Vision Circles represent the primary ways of processing information which develop naturally during early childhood: *builder, observer, communicator, resonator, nurturer, synergist, animator and internaliser.*

MORE TO EXPLORE

Paul DENNISON, Gail DENNISON **Brain Gym** and **Brain Gym, teacher's edition** Edu-Kinesthetics Inc 1989. *Illustrations and simplified instructions for doing each exercise, for use with children. Teacher's book gives teaching tips, variations and benefits.*

Carla HANNAFORD **Smart Moves – why learning is not all in your head** Great Ocean Publishers 1995. *Information about the body's role in learning and how the two hemispheres of the brain work together – with a chapter on Brain Gym.*

Carla HANNAFORD **The Dominance Factor – how knowing your dominant eye, ear, brain, hand and foot can improve your learning** Great Ocean Publishers 1997. *Discover your learning profile, why some people naturally find it easier to learn than others, and how to help those others.*

Sharon PROMISLOW **Making the Brain-Body Connection** Kinetic Publishing Corporation 1999. *Clear, readable information about how your brain and body are interconnected with lots of activities for building the connections and improving learning (including information on Brain Gym).*

www.braingym.org, www.braingym.org.uk Brain Gym® organisation

www.quantumcoaching.co.uk *Sports coaching for R/L balance*

www.vision-training.com *Improving vision naturally*

Non-Conscious Processing

Most traditional education and academic 'teaching', is directed at the conscious mind. Study is valued. Learning is hard, but if we persevere and if we have the right sort of mind, we'll get there in the end. Guess what. This only happens when children go to school. Until then, children learn from the vast soup of unsimplified input all around them, and some part of them chooses what it is they need to learn – and they learn it.

The human being, made up of mind, body, emotion, spirit, is designed to learn effortlessly. We are presented with information, we try things out, we notice the response we get and either continue doing the same thing or do something different in order to get a different response. 'Mistakes' are simply feedback – an essential part of the learning process. But that's when we're learning 'naturally' – or non-consciously – things that we 'need' to know.

Because we are conscious only of what we are conscious of, we tend to think that conscious awareness is all there is. And yet if we really look at our lives, decisions we have made, and how we have learnt most things, we become aware of how much has been influenced by things beyond our conscious control. The mind can be likened to an iceberg. We are taking in information through our senses all the time (represented by the vast majority of the iceberg below the surface), but at any one moment, only a very small fraction of that information is brought to our conscious awareness ('the tip of the iceberg'). The conscious and the non-conscious minds work in very different ways (see table next page). Traditionally we take a 'top down' approach when we teach to the conscious mind, but the way human beings learn naturally is through a bottom-up approach – we take in large amounts of information non-consciously and those things which are of importance rise to conscious awareness when we need them.

The real way to teach to the non-conscious mind is to give learners access to as many interesting activities as possible and leave it to them to learn what they need to learn. For those who work within a more formal structure, though, there are still things that can be done to make learning easier by stimulating the non-conscious mind.

TERMINOLOGY

Conscious – 'normal' state of being awake and aware

Pre-conscious – term used by Norman Dixon to describe the state of the mind and body in the fraction of a second before we start to act or think consciously

Subconscious – those things just below the surface of our conscious awareness

Unconscious – much deeper, less accessible memories and influences (I avoid this term because of its associations with certain schools of psychotherapy, and of being knocked out)

Paraconscious – term used by Georgi Lozanov to describe the state of normal awareness which does not require careful thought when we are most receptive to learning – the relaxed unfocused state of listening to music while we're ironing, for example; this is the state most of the suggestions in this chapter are attempting to access

Non-conscious – general term used here to describe 'other than conscious', rather than trying to differentiate between any of the specific states mentioned above

---

PERIPHERAL LEARNING

We notice all sorts of things going on around us without conscious awareness – and the non-conscious picks up subtle signals much more than the obvious ones.

- *Decorate the walls. Have a varied display of items which are visually pleasing and interesting in their own right. We learn best things which interest us or which we like – pictures, cartoons, jokes, quotations, interesting stories, etc. Within the display include lots of real-life examples of material recently covered and about to be covered in the coursebook. Encourage students to add their own contributions.*

LEARNING ENVIRONMENT

The learning environment (page 41) is of great importance because both the physical environment and the attitude and behaviour of the teacher are some of the peripheral information being taken in by the non-conscious mind.

BIG PICTURE

The non-conscious mind likes to have the big picture before going into detail.

- *Let learners know where they're going. Give them your plans for the session, the week, the term … or from now until the exam. Write it up in black and white, possibly as a mindmap, and colour it in to show progress.*
- *If you're using a coursebook, spend time getting to know it.*

Ask questions to help students find out what's on different pages, in different units or sections.

OVERLOAD

The non-conscious mind needs a lot of information in order to perceive patterns and make sense of it. Don't be afraid to use long stories and unsimplified materials. The emphasis here needs to be on large amounts of receptive information, without pressure to produce.

- *Try starting at the back of the book with the final unit and work backwards to the beginning. Your lessons get easier and easier rather than more and more difficult. Use the earlier parts of the book for reference to enable you to deal with more complicated material. After the initial surprise, learners rise to the challenge and you get through the book much more quickly and efficiently.*

NEED

The non-conscious mind looks for things that it needs. Need means immediate need for the human organism. A distant examination doesn't count – although an exam next week might! But one of the real difficulties about learning something in school or in a training session, or just because you think it would be nice, is that the non-conscious mind knows there's no urgency about it and therefore doesn't make it a priority. So we have to find ways of creating perceived need to learn.

CONSCIOUS	NON-CONSCIOUS
Active and controlling	Receptive, spontaneous, participatory
Part analysis; build from part to whole (focus on separate units)	Whole comes first; from whole to part (interconnection, patterns, fields)
Low volume, reductive	High volume
Specifics, exactness	Ambiguity
Interpretation, consistency	Incorporates new material
Right/wrong; obsession with correctness	Errors are learning material
Machine-like fixed approach; attachment to the status quo	Organic plasticity; let it emerge
Analytical, going deeper into detail	Creative, looking for new relationships
Does it make sense?	Does it give pleasure?
High focus, concentration	Relaxation
Competitive (separating/ranking)	Co-operation, bonding is first impulse
Mental dominant	Holistic – feeling, sensation, intuition dominant
Objective	Subjective
Serial function	Parallel function

From 'The Quantum Revolution in Education: Organic Learning' by Grethe Hooper Hansen in Proceedings of 9th International SEAL Conference 2001: *Opening Minds to Holistic Learning*

- *Asking questions, using real materials and letting learners choose projects of interest to themselves will create more of a perceived need to learn than spoon-feeding them with information.*
- *Let learners choose what they want to learn.*

PLEASURE

The non-conscious mind looks for things it enjoys.

- *Use material and subjects of intrinsic interest to people. Let them bring in their own materials or work on specific projects of their choice. Not everyone has to use the same material at the same time.*
- *Do activities which are fun and interesting. Songs, rhymes, games, stories and projects do help non-conscious as well as conscious learning. Make sure that you don't destroy the pleasure by following every pleasurable activity with searching questions on which learners are going to be judged.*

SELF-DISCOVERY

The mind likes to find 'the answer' – but when it does, it immediately moves on to the next 'challenge' or unanswered question. As we all know, understanding something is not the same as remembering it, but what is not so well known is that understanding something too quickly can make it much more difficult to remember. It is therefore important to ask questions rather than give too many answers. By telling learners information, we are effectively robbing them of it.

- *Ask questions for students to discover their own answers. Don't worry if learners don't 'get it' immediately. Material that we have discovered for ourselves is much more memorable. So is information that we come to after a longer period of discovery. The non-conscious mind makes its own sense of material: chaos and the temporary frustration of incomprehension can lead to more retained knowledge in the long run.*

TIME

While the conscious mind looks for solutions and action, the non-conscious mind works better given time. Have you noticed how the answers to problems often pop into your mind after a good night's sleep or while you're in the bath? That's the 'bottom-up' approach in action. How can you access it?

- *Leave questions and problems open for a period of time – preferably until a following session. Leave processing time between giving new information and asking learners to answer questions about it.*
- *Spend a few minutes previewing homework in class, so that by the time learners come to do it, they will find it easier because their non-conscious will have been working on it. (This is effective when doing your own tasks too.)*

> By telling learners information, we are effectively robbing them of it.

METAPHOR

Metaphors and stories (page 26) are both 'weak signals' and contain unanswered questions – manna to the non-conscious.

CREATIVITY

More learning comes from creative activities (page 35) than from sterile exercises. Poetry, creative writing, producing and performing short plays, songs and raps, playing with language, producing a newspaper, etc, are all effective. Producing the work for display, performance or in-house publication creates the need for editing and rehearsal, so we are not talking about creativity at the expense of accuracy. Art and dance are also conducive to learning.

CO-OPERATION

The non-conscious mind likes to co-operate, not compete. Although a degree of competition can be

---

Come to your senses

The **eye** takes in **10 million** bits of information per second and deals consciously with **40.**

The **ear** takes in **100,000** bits of information per second and can deal consciously with **30.**

The **skin** takes in **100,000** bits of information per second and can deal consciously with **5.**

We can **smell 100,000** bits of information per second and can deal consciously with **one.**

We can **taste 1,000** bits of information per second and can deal consciously with **one.**

From **Human Physiology** by Manfred Zimmermann's Springer-Verlag 1989.

fun, it's most fun for the winners but there are many more losers than winners. There are lots of activities and games which are just as much fun if everyone wins. Competition can be encouraged as competition against oneself – over a period of time learning to do things better than you could do them before – rather than competition with other learners. Everyone who shows improvement should be acknowledged, rather than limiting praise to those who do better than others.

SUCCESS

It is important to set up an atmosphere where errors really are viewed as an essential part of the learning process and an opportunity to improve without the stigma attached to failure. (Failure is very much a conscious mind concept and can lead to 'self-consciousness' and withdrawal from situations of risk.) This means reducing testing and competition to a minimum and focusing on teaching, experimenting and playing. Focus instead on success, improvement and those things people do well.

> Whether you think you can or think you can't, you're right.
>
> HENRY FORD

RELAXATION

The natural learning state of the non-conscious mind is one of relaxed alertness, free from stress. So once again, reducing testing and the possibility of failure is essential, while creating an enjoyable, positive atmosphere of learning in the classroom with activities of intrinsic interest and without pressure to perform. It can also be helpful to teach and practise simple relaxation and meditation techniques (page 39). In order to be relaxed, we need to be physically, mentally and emotionally comfortable. So acknowledge emotions (the teacher's as well as the learners'), and encourage learners to express their emotions.

DIRECT ACCESS

Many other techniques appeal directly to the non-conscious mind. One is PhotoReading (page 77). For another, '21-21', see the box below.

RELATIONSHIP

Possibly the biggest impact teachers and trainers can have on students' learning is through the relationship they have with the students. Research shows that if people are treated with respect by people who are passionate about their subject, they are more disposed to learn. The reason this comes under the heading of 'non-conscious learning' is that this is not something you can fake. The non-conscious mind picks up on the subtle, non-verbal signals you are sending out, through your body language and tone of voice, as well as the words you use. So genuine respect means really taking the time to listen to students (possibly first having taken time to prove to them that you really do want to listen to them) and then being prepared to take account of what they say.

❋ ❋ ❋

I certainly do not want to imply that there is no place for the conscious mind in learning. It is the part of the mind that allows us to plan, prioritise and act; to override our emotional responses so we can interact in a 'civilised' way – and to suppress information or emotions that might stop us from acting, and which can thereby inhibit learning. I suggest only that we redress the balance. Where we have traditionally only taught to the conscious mind, by paying more attention to the non-conscious messages we are giving students, we will release more of our natural ability to learn quickly and easily.

Special thanks to Grethe Hooper Hansen for many of the ideas on the non-conscious which are dealt with in greater detail in her forthcoming book, **Undermind**.

MORE TO EXPLORE

Norman DIXON **Preconscious Processing** John Wiley & Sons 1981. *Important understandings but not an easy read.*

Grethe HOOPER HANSEN **Undermind** 2004. *Understandings and practical implications of the non-conscious in learning.*

21-21

- Choose a statement related to a positive response to learning, eg *I can learn maths quickly and easily*.
- Each day for 21 days, sit quietly and write the statement 21 times.
- As you write, notice any thoughts or feelings that arise. These can frequently give you insights into aspects of your mind that might be resisting the learning process, and may cause you to change the sentence, for example, to *'I deserve to learn maths quickly and easily.'*

Story, Metaphor and Visualisation

Once upon a time there was a tribe that forgot its stories, and the world became dull, dull, dull. And the people knew there was something missing from their lives, so they made up rules and found that if they worked very hard and didn't think too much, they could pretend that everything was all right. And this went on so long that they began to think this was how it had always been. So when the children tried to play, the adults no longer recognised the stories, and made the children play by their rules. (*Finish the story for yourself.*)

Most people spend much of their lives living in a fantasy world. Is it just to escape? Or is it because stories are our natural way of making sense of the world and transmitting information? Think about it: fairy tales, soap operas, novels and fiction of all kinds in books, radio, TV and films, religious parables, fables, scientific hypotheses, models of reality. They're all stories. And the same is true in all cultures. Before the printing press was invented, stories were the way people passed their knowledge and culture orally from one generation to the next. Why? Because stories enable us to 'get our heads round' 'reality' – and they are so much more memorable than straight facts.

> *What is your metaphor for learning?*

MEMES

Cultural evolution cannot be explained by genetic and biological evolution, and yet culture does evolve. Richard Dawkins proposed that it evolved through songs, fashions, stories, facts and ideas, and just as biological evolution is carried in genes and the genome, so he coined the word 'meme' to mean 'a unit of cultural transmission'. So a meme can be anything which carries cultural information, from catchphrases, a line of a poem, a film, an item of clothing that 'catches on' – to stories of all kinds.

At a higher level, value memes (Vmemes) are the organising principles which structure how people think and behave.

Our job as teachers is to offer students questions, give them access to lots of information, distract their conscious minds, and let their non-conscious minds sort out the answers. The non-conscious mind loves stories. Metaphors (something representing something else) and stories are an excellent vehicle for imparting such information – language, ideas, moral messages, values and beliefs, embedded suggestions, and of course historical, scientific or geographical facts.

And it's better if you don't spell out the meaning at the end – Aesop take note! So be careful to retain the essential element of enjoyment. It isn't necessary to dissect stories or ask a lot of questions 'to make sure students have understood' – or if you do, do it later when the non-conscious mind has had time to work on it.

METAPHOR

Our everyday speech is littered with metaphor. We are *'attacked'* by viruses, *'shoot down'* ideas, *'get all hot under the collar'*, *'go off in the wrong direction'*, or *'round in circles'*, feel *'high'*, *'low'* or *'blue'*, *'spend'* time … the list is endless. What do you as a teacher think when a student says *'it's like banging my head against a brick wall'*, or *'I've got knots (or butterflies) in my stomach'*, or *'I've got the weight of the world on my shoulders'*? We understand things better by comparing them with other things. But it's more than that. The metaphors we use show how we are relating to the world. And it's alarming how many of our everyday metaphors relate to violence and war, with our *'plans of attack'*, *'defence of our positions'*, and *'going for the jugular'*! Change your metaphors, change the way you think about things. Try the metaphor of gardening for teaching: *sowing seeds, nurturing, preparing fertile ground, blossoming ideas ...*

- As well as directly exploring this rich vein of enquiry, you might profit from thinking of your metaphor for teaching. And for learning. How similar are they?
- Or take an object at random (a paperclip, a bunch of grapes, a key) and see how many ways you

can find to compare it with your chosen topic. What light does it shine? What insights do you get?

- Ask students for their metaphors. Which animal is most representative of them? Or of the school or organisation?

> Which of these jobs is most like your metaphor for being a teacher?
>
> | *Sports coach* | *Nurse* | *Sergeant major* |
> |---|---|---|
> | *Psychotherapist* | *Comedian* | *Lecturer* |
> | *Police officer* | *Paid companion* | *Actor* |
> | *Slave* | *Inventor* | *Artist* |
>
> In what ways is each of these like a teacher?
>
> Can you think of other jobs or roles which are more relevant?

'Stories don't have a middle and an end,' said Stephen Spielberg. *'They usually have a beginning that never stops beginning.'* Once you start exploring stories as a way of teaching, you never stop beginning.

VISUALISATION

Visualisation is using your imagination to make 'images' inside your head. For some people these are clear pictures, for others it's a kind of smudgy

> *The essence of metaphor is understanding and experiencing one kind of thing in terms of another.*
> LAKOFF AND JOHNSON IN METAPHORS WE LIVE BY

impression (page 66). But everyone can visualise, and we do it all the time to anticipate a variety of possible futures so that we can make necessary preparations. Of course, many of these preparations happen non-consciously and when we actively 'do visualisations' in a relaxed state (when the mind is most susceptible to suggestion) it is the non-conscious mind we are trying to activate.

Classic guided visualisations take the form of some sort of journey, possibly with meeting a wise person or a guardian (actually an inner part of yourself) who may give you a gift (something you need). Visualisation is also recognised as being a powerful healing force. Try visualising the release of tension and bringing in healing energy for yourself – or visualising healing for other people.

Many top athletes believe in the power of visualisation. In the 1984 Olympics, American gymnast Mary Lou Retton was about to do her final vault. She had to get a perfect score for the gold medal. She closed her eyes for a few seconds, then got into position – and got her perfect score. When she closed her eyes, she told reporters afterwards, she was visualising herself doing every motion perfectly.

American professional tennis player and coach Timothy Gallwey identified the 'inner game' in the mind of the player as a more powerful determinant of success than the outer game. His method involves recognising the potential conflict between two selves, and to change habits by achieving a state of relaxed concentration, using observation, visualisation, 'feelmages' and goal-setting (self 2), rather than by verbally disciplining ourselves (self 1). Once the basic moves have been learnt, players have to respond at a much faster rate than the conscious mind can cope with. It is therefore the non-conscious that is being 'trained' through visualisation.

> *We play the Inner Game the day we realise that the opponent in our own head is more daunting than the one on the other side of the net.*
> TIMOTHY GALLWEY

In Accelerated Learning, many use this powerful tool to aid learning too. An important practical aspect is to visualise positively what you do want, and not to focus on what you don't want, since the non-conscious mind focuses on images, not words, and therefore does not recognise the negative (try yourself to imagine what 'not a pink elephant' looks like).

EXTELLIGENCE

Extelligence is the intelligence we share. Where intelligence refers to a single being, extelligence is external and shared, with new knowledge being created in the interaction of of the two – of a brain with a book, or another brain. Extelligence can be viewed as the sum of all the stories we have invented so far. We can see how extelligence can be created in discourse, how we use it as a fundamental way of getting about, working together and 'knowing' things. And this brings about even more extelligence. The internet is bringing about a huge blossoming in extelligence today.

Ian Stewart and Jack Cohen, who coined the term, suggest that intelligence and extelligence may have co-evolved. Brains developed when they had something to be intelligent about, and writing, speaking and other extelligence must surely be developed in parallel. The idea of extelligence leads us to view learning in terms of developing narratives, endlessly re-shaped and shared in public, as opposed to a private and solely internal process.

Contributed by Mark McKergow

MORE TO EXPLORE

STORY AND METAPHOR

George LAKOFF and Mark JOHNSON **Metaphors We Live By** The University of Chicago Press 1980. *How metaphors define the realities we live by as shown by the language we use.*

James LAWLEY and Penny TOMPKINS **Metaphors in Mind** The Developing Company Press 2000. *Symbolic Modelling from David Grove's Clean Language, for therapists and teachers.*

Nick OWEN **The Magic of Metaphor – 77 stories for teachers, trainers & thinkers** Crown House Publishing 2001. *Stories and advice.*

Jack CANFIELD and Mark Victor HANSEN **Chicken Soup for the Soul - 101 stories to open the heart and rekindle the spirit** Health Communications Inc 1993. *Inspirational stories.*

S MACCUSH, M PATEL, A WELLS **The Flame that Transforms – 60 empowering stories of hope, courage and inspiration** Life Foundation Publications 2003. *Inspirational stories.*

VISUALISATION

Carl SIMONTON, Stephanie MATTHEWS SIMONTON, James CREIGHTON **Getting Well Again** Bantam 1992. *Overcoming cancer, largely through visualisation.*

Timothey GALLWEY **The Inner Game of Tennis** Pan 1986. *Using visualisation to succeed in tennis. (Also available for other sports.)*

EXTELLIGENCE

Terry PRATCHETT, Ian STEWART & Jack COHEN **The Science of Discworld** and **The Science of Discworld II: The Globe** Ebury Press 2002. *Book one: the origins and development of our universe and extelligence. Book two: the development of everything that makes us human.*

Richard DAWKINS **The Selfish Gene** Oxford Press 1990. *The book which proposed the concept of the 'meme'.*

Multiple Intelligences

Howard Gardner put forward the theory of Multiple Intelligences in his book *Frames of Mind* (first published 1983, revised edition 1993) to challenge the validity of IQ as the basis of assessment. Gardner proposes that there are numerous qualities which can be termed 'intelligences'; that these can grow and develop; and that intelligence, in its broadest sense, can be an indicator of potential. The basic MI message is that things we have traditionally classified as 'talents' (she's good at dancing, he's a natural footballer) should be valued as much as IQ which is basically only the talent for academic learning.

MI theory is simply that – a scientific theory. It does not directly translate into classroom practice. However, Gardner himself suggests that it has two implications:

1 Individuality. We should know as much as possible about each person so they can learn, and demonstrate their learning in ways which are comfortable to them.
2 Values. The intelligences themselves are amoral. How anyone teaches and what they do in the classroom is/should be based on their values and what is important to them.

Although people who are differentially intelligent are likely to learn in different ways, MI theory does not directly correlate with a person's learning style (page 33), nor is it about testing, classifying and labelling people under yet more headings. It's about appreciating people for who they are and for all the things they are good at.

> *Gardner's definition of an intelligence:*
> *a biophysical potential to process information in certain ways in order to solve problems or fashion products that are valued in a culture or community*

MI theory does, of course, have implications for assessment, curriculum and pedagogy and many other people have translated the MI theory into classroom practice. Gardner's own ideas about teaching are set out in his other books – *The Unschooled Mind, The Disciplined Mind* and, most recently, the co-authored *Good Work*, which emphasises the importance of living and acting with integrity. One thing he is clear on: MI Theory is not an educational goal in itself. It is not enough to say 'I have done all the intelligences' (whatever that means). It is important to know for what purpose the theory is being used.

Thanks to Howard Gardner for reading and commenting on this section.

INTELLIGENCE QUOTIENT (IQ)

The IQ test was devised in the early 1900s by Alfred Binet and Théodore Simon as a way of weeding out retarded children and placing the remainder at the appropriate level in schools. It was therefore a test of suitability for school more than 100 years ago, and even today a high IQ indicates whether someone is suited to an academic life. The test does not show suitability for leadership, commerce, politics, manual skills, agriculture, the caring professions, the arts or sport – all essential in a healthy society.

The IQ test is based on two forms of intelligence, logical-mathematical and verbal-linguistic, with a strong cultural bias. It tests discrete items unrelated to one another or to everyday life. It assumes that intelligence is fixed, without potential for development. It is a test of learning up to that point and not an indicator of future performance. It also tests product, not process – there is no indication of how an answer is arrived at, or whether the process is transferable. Ultimately it is very unfair.

Howard Gardner's Multiple Intelligences

Gardner's original seven intelligences are:
- **Visual-spatial**
- **Bodily-kinaesthetic**
- **Verbal-linguistic**
- **Musical**
- **Mathematical-logical**
- **Intrapersonal (knowledge of self)**
- **Interpersonal (awareness of others)**

He later added an eighth, the **naturalist** intelligence which is about having an affinity with nature and also being able to categorise.

He is currently testing the presence of another intelligence, which he calls 'number eight and a half', the **existential** intelligence, ie a capacity to contemplate the 'big' philosophical questions, such as 'Why are we here?' 'What is the purpose of life?' (He specifically rejects the notion of a 'spiritual' intelligence.)

MULTIPLICITY OF INTELLIGENCES

Gardner acknowledges, although he does not specifically comment on, the concept of an MI profile, also called a multiplicity of intelligences. This is based on the understanding that each intelligence category actually covers a range of different skills and abilities. For example, music is made up of rhythm, tone, pitch, notation, playing a range of different instruments, singing, etc. Any one person will have different levels of skill in each of these aspects, and we all have potential in them all, but to different degrees. Potential may be enhanced or lost depending on how much we practise and develop each aspect, and Gardner does say that intelligences are to be developed. He has not yet said how, but just 'doing a bit of movement' and 'playing a bit of music' isn't it!

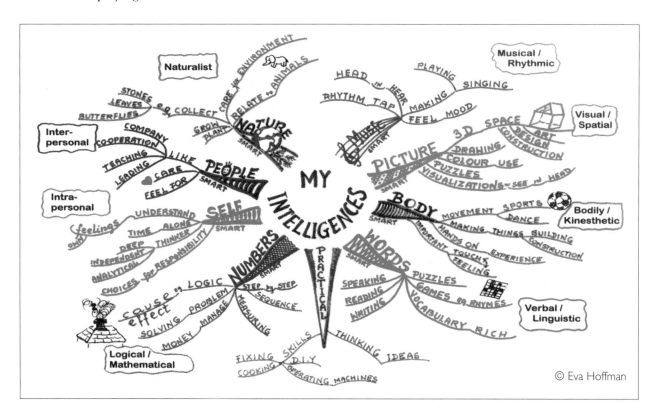

© Eva Hoffman

BUZAN

Tony Buzan, inventor of mind maps, takes a different approach. He also uses the word 'intelligence' to describe different aspects of personal development. He provides a series of questionnaires to determine strengths and weaknesses across the range of the different aspects of each intelligence, and then activities and exercises to help build strengths in areas which are not so strong. The aim is for most people to become capable in all fields.

His classifications are:

- **Creative**
- **Personal**
- **Social**
- **Spiritual**
- **Physical**
- **Sensual**
- **Sexual**
- **Numerical**
- **Spatial**
- **Verbal**

> *75% of presenters are sequential, analytical presenters – that's how their lesson is organized ... yet 100% of their participants are multi-processors*
>
> ERIC JENSEN

HOFFMAN

Eva Hoffman has also written about MI and done much to make it understood in schools. The thrust of her work is to make learners, especially children, aware of their learning styles and their many intelligences, so they learn to value themselves and others for their uniqueness and individuality, and also have the tools to take responsibility for their own learning. The mind map (previous page) shows her own classifications (she has changed some of Gardner's names to make them more accessible), with the addition of her own proposed 'practical intelligence' (Gardner's eight are indicated in the outer boxes). She also offers a tenth intelligence, the 'spiritual intelligence', but it is not included in the mindmap so that teachers can decide whether to present it or not.

> *Gardner has changed the question from 'How intelligent are you?' to 'In what ways are you intelligent?'*

MORE TO EXPLORE

MULTIPLE INTELLIGENCES

Howard GARDNER **Frames of Mind** Fontana Press (HarperCollins) 1983, 1993. *The original book proposing the theory.*

Howard GARDNER **The Unschooled Mind – how children think and how schools should teach** Basic Books1995 and **The Disciplined Mind: beyond facts and standardized tests, the K-12 education that every child deserves** Penguin USA 2000. *Gardner's own practical implications of the theory for schools.*

Howard GARDNER, Mihaly CSIKSZENTMIHALYI, William DAMON **Good Work – when excellence and ethics meet** Basic Books 2001. *The importance of values to inform MI theory.*

Tony BUZAN **Head First** Thorsons (HarperCollins) 2000. *Exercises and questionnaires to assess and develop personal skills.*

Eva HOFFMAN **Introducing Children to their Intelligences** Learn to Learn 2001. *A step-by-step photocopiable resource which teaches children about their intelligences and learning.*

Dr Spencer KAGAN, Miguel KAGAN **Multiple Intelligences** Kagan Cooperative Learning 1998. *A huge resource of information about MI (many more than Gardner's eight), and many practical activities for schools.*

EMOTIONAL INTELLIGENCE *(see next page)*

Daniel GOLEMAN **Emotional Intelligence; why it can matter more than IQ** Bantam Books 1995. *Clearest investigation of EQ.*

Patrick E MERLEVEDE, Denis BRIDOUX, Rudy VANDAMME **7 Steps to Emotional Intelligence** Crown House Publishing 1997. *Practical activities from NLP to develop emotional intelligence.*

Candace PERT **Molecules of Emotion** Scribner 1997. *A neuroscientist gives the biomolecular basis of emotions.*

Joseph LEDOUX **The Emotional Brain** Weidenfeld & Nicolson 1998. *Proof that fear is linked with the amygdala in the brain.*

www.antidote.org.uk *Introducing emotional literacy into Uk schools.*

SPIRITUAL INTELLIGENCE *(see next page)*

Danah ZOHAR, Ian MARSHALL **SQ: The Ultimate Intelligence** Bloomsbury 2001. *The first book directly addressing SQ. Also* **The Quantum Soul** HarperCollins 2004 *(forthcoming)*

Eckhart TOLLE **The Power of Now** and **Practising The Power of Now** Hodder & Stoughton 1999/2001. *Practical spirituality.*

Tony BUZAN **The Power of Spiritual Intelligence** Thorsons 2001. *Ten ways to tap into your spiritual genius.*

Dalai Lama **The Art of Happiness: A Handbook for Living** Hodder & Stoughton 1999. *Spiritual living.*

Michal LEVIN **Spiritual Intelligence – awakening the power of your spirituality and intuition** Hodder & Stoughton 2000. *Explanation and starting point for inner exploration.*

Danna BEAL **Tragedy in the Workplace** Danna Beal Consulting 2000. *Building emotional and spiritual competence in business.*

Georgeanne LAMONT **The Spirited Business – success stories of soul-friendly companies** Hodder & Stoughton 2002. *Practical steps for introducing spirituality into business – with examples.*

Sally BURNS, Georgeanne LAMONT **Values and Visions – a handbook for spiritual development and global awareness** Hodder & Stoughton 1993. *Practical activities for school use.*

EMOTIONAL INTELLIGENCE

EQ – emotional quotient or emotional intelligence – came into popular consciousness with the publication of the book by Daniel Goleman. He presents a combination of Gardner's two personal intelligences – intrapersonal and interpersonal (which Gardner also presents as being very closely linked). EQ is about knowing yourself and knowing how you interact with others.

In western societies, we are traditionally not good at knowing our emotions or expressing them. Emotions can be one of the biggest blocks to learning, and, conversely, one needs to be in a good emotional state in order to be in a good state for learning (pages 16 and 37). It is therefore of crucial importance that we address the question of EQ. Teachers and trainers need to acknowledge their own emotions and those of the learners. We need to teach children – and adults – to recognise, accept and express their emotions, both positive and negative, without blame, as a necessary first step to being able to control them to an acceptable degree in social situations. Indeed most people need to learn that they are not totally controlled by their emotions, but can override them on a temporary basis, although for emotional well-being it is important in the long-term to deal with the issues at the source of negative emotions. But this is a learning process, with allowable mistakes along the way. Too often in schools we try to go straight to the control of emotions, which simply leads to suppression – with the result that negative emotions often emerge as disruptive behaviour.

....

SPIRITUAL INTELLIGENCE

The existence of Spiritual Intelligence has been proposed by many people, especially Danah Zohar. Does it need teaching? It certainly needs acknowledging so that people are at least aware that there's an alternative to a purely materialist view which doesn't depend on organised religion.

Spirituality is not to be confused with religion or religions, which are social constructs designed to foster spiritual experience. People with strong religious beliefs usually have a channel for their spirituality. But people in 'general' can have their spirituality acknowledged without being tied to any specific religion, belief or faith, possibly through philosophy ... and also through meditation, relaxation and quiet time.

Spiritual enlightenment seems to be very much bound up with true happiness and a consensus view seems to be that becoming emotionally competent, meditation (page 39) and being 'nice' to oneself and others are the first practical steps one can take. The important thing is that spirituality is something that can be lived on an everyday basis. It is a practical approach to living well.

EIGHT TOOLS OF REFLECTION
Stillness
Listening
Story
Encounter
Celebration
Grieving
Visioning
Journalling
The practical tools for introducing spirituality into business.
From **The Spirited Business** by Georgeanne Lamont

Learning Styles

A person's learning style is to do with how they innately learn best – and there are many models of human behaviour which can help us understand factors which might affect that. The **VAK** model from NLP (page 62), which is probably one of the most useful areas for teachers to consider in terms of the way they teach, indicates a person's sensory preferences for taking in information, processing information and recalling information. The preference which has traditionally been overlooked is kinesthetic – the need for touch, movement and emotional impact. This is unfortunate, since it is the modality which is most effective for most people when it comes to long-term learning.

The **metaprogram** model from NLP (page 65) also gives important indicators about how people are motivated and some of their behavioural preferences, and numerous other models indicate how people develop individually and interact with one another (which will affect how they learn): **Transactional Analysis** (page 71), the **Belbin Team Role Analysis** (page 74), the **Myers Briggs Type Indicator** (page 73), the **Enneagram** (page 72), **Spiral Dynamics** (page 69) and the **Seven Levels of Conciousness Model** (page 70). And there are many more. Howard Gardner's **Multiple Intelligence theory** (page 29) has implications for testing, the curriculum and pedagogy, although it does not directly relate to learning styles.

HONEY AND MUMFORD'S LEARNING STYLES PROFILE

Each individual's profile, developed by Peter Honey and Alan Mumford. indicates strong, medium or low preferences for each of the four different styles of learning. The sample profile shows someone with a strong Activist preference and medium Pragmatist (solid lines) plotted against accepted norms (dotted lines).

Activist
Hands-on learner. Likes trial and error.
Probable likes: *brainstorming, problem solving, discussions, puzzles, roleplay, competitions*

Reflector
'Tell me.' Likes to receive information.
Probable likes: *discussions, questionnaires, observing, time out, coaching, interviews*

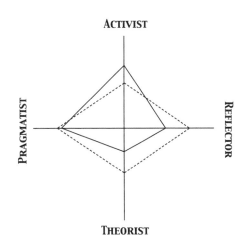

Theorist
'Convince me.' Likes reassurance of relevance.
Probable likes: *models, statistics, stories, quotes, information, theories*

Pragmatist
'Show me.' Likes demonstrations from experts
Probable likes: *time to think, case studies, discussions, problem solving*

MORE TO EXPLORE
Peter HONEY and Alan MUMFORD **Using Your Learning Styles** Peter Honey 1983
www.peterhoney.com
www.ruby3.dircon.co.uk

Learning Theories

Here are two other learning theories which should not be omitted, plus some other thoughts on learning.

UNCONSCIOUS COMPETENCE

Flow – the skill is used without conscious attention

CONSCIOUS COMPETENCE

I know that I know.
Practice – attention and mistakes.

CONSCIOUS INCOMPETENCE

I know that I don't know.
I start doing something about it.

UNCONSCIOUS INCOMPETENCE

I don't know that I don't know.

The Chinese symbol for learning is made up of two concepts:
studying
and
practising constantly
It's an on-going verb.

Learning is finding out what you already know.
Doing is demonstrating that you know it.
Teaching is reminding others that they know it just as well as you.
We are all learners, doers, teachers.

RICHARD BACH

KOLB'S EXPERIENTIAL LEARNING CYCLE

David Kolb and Roger Fry's model shows the four learning styles which correspond to the two phases of the learning cycle closest to them.

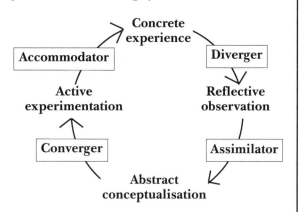

RACE'S EXPERIENTIAL LEARNING CYCLE

Philip Race's four learning processes interact with one another like ripples in a pond, rather than following a cycle. The starting point is 'wanting to learn'.

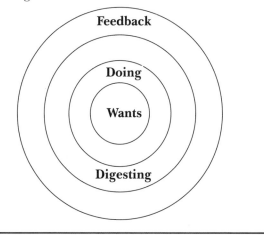

MORE TO EXPLORE

Michael GELB, Tony BUZAN **Lessons from the Art of Juggling – how to achieve your full potential in business, learning and life** Crown trade Paperbacks 1994. *Wonderful exploration of the learning process. Learning to juggle is good too.*

www.algonquin.on.ca/edtech/gened/styles.html *Learning styles, Kolb, Race and more.*

www.infed.org *Encyclopedia of learning.*

Creativity and Thinking Skills

Many of the 'right-brain' approaches lead to creative thinking – getting away from the left-brain logical step-by-step approach. Here are some pointers to thinking 'outside the box'.

ROGER VON OECH

Von Oech recommends lots of practical ways to use your 'explorer', 'artist', 'judge' and 'warrior' to be more creative. The explorer is looking at the big picture in new ways. The artist is asked how to change an idea by changing the way of thinking. How can you: *adapt, imagine, reverse, connect, compare, eliminate, parody* or *incubate* the idea? The judge evaluates an idea and decides what to do with it. The warrior carries the idea into action.

> *People who are only good with hammers see every problem as a nail.*
>
> ABRAHAM MASLOW

How many uses can you think of for a paper clip?

When you run out of initial ideas, think of how many things a paper clip cannot be used for.

Go through this second list and find creative ways to use a paper clip to fulfil each purpose. You can be creative in your definition of the word 'paper clip'.

'OUTSIDE THE BOX' THINKING

Join these nine dots with four straight lines without taking your pen from the paper.

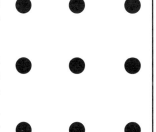

Easy? Then how about getting more creative and finding as many ways as possible to join all nine dots with only one line?

Answers at www.seal.org.uk

EDWARD DE BONO

Edward De Bono has developed many ways of teaching people to think more creatively. His concept of 'lateral thinking' involves thinking in ways other than logically, the classic problem being a lorry stuck under a bridge. While the adults are looking at the roof stuck against the bridge, it is a child's 'lateral' suggestion to let some air out of the tyres that frees it.

De Bono has introduced numerous ideas to 'unstick' thinking. One is the 'PMI' – look for the Plus, Minus, and Interesting points about a range of different suggestions, which might lead to acceptance of an existing proposal or to insight into a totally new idea. Another is the 'Six Thinking Hats'. Each hat represent a different style of thinking, each of which has a positive role in creative thinking, problem-solving and decision-making.

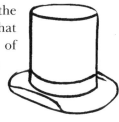

White   Facts, objectivity, neutral thinking
Green   Creativity, new ideas
Yellow Positive thinking, making ideas work
Black   Negative thinking, looking for problems
Red   Emotional reaction, feeling response
Blue   Control of other styles, chairperson

> *Nothing is more dangerous than an idea when it is the only one you have.*
>
> EMILE CHARTIER, FRENCH PHILOSOPHER

MORE TO EXPLORE

Edward DE BONO **Lateral Thinking** Penguin 1970; **Six Thinking Hats** Viking 1985. *All De Bono's books offer new ways of developing thinking skills.*

Roger VAN OECH **A Whack on the Side of the Head** Angus and Robertson 1983; **A Kick in the Seat of the Pants** Harper and Row 1986; also **Creative Whack Pack** US Games Systems 1992. *'Kick in the pants' in card format.*

Robert FISHER **Teaching Children to Think** Stanley Thornes 1990

See also **TOC** (page 75), **Solutions Focus** (page 76) and **Rhizomatic Learning** (page 78)

Memory

In ancient Greek and Roman times, memory was greatly valued – the word itself comes from the name of the Greek goddess of memory, Mnemosyne. Roman senators had to address the senate without written notes, so they perfected ways of improving their memories, and identified the two main principles underlying conscious memory: **imagination** and **association**. You associate the thing you want to remember with something fixed, and then you use your imagination to make the picture as vivid as possible. The Romans associated their ideas with fixed points around the room they were talking in, and then referred to them (which gives the English expressions: *In the first place …, in the second place …*, etc.)

> *As you get older, three things go. The first is your memory … and I can't remember the other two.*
>
> NORMAN WISDOM IN HIS 80s

> *All the things which are good and bad for the brain (page 15) similarly aid or hinder memory.*

The peg-word and link-word systems involve learning a series of items linked to numbers (1=sun, 2=shoe, etc, or a phonetic system which can run into the thousands). This is the list to which you then 'peg' the items you wish to remember by creating vivid images involving the peg word and the item to be remembered. Alternatively create a story in which a series of items are linked sequentially.

Of course, the Suggestopedic method (page 47) is designed so that learners remember without effort or needing to use systems.

We remember

- information important for our survival
- what we find meaningful
- what we give attention to
- what we practise
- what we link to things we already know
- what we encode using mnemonics, etc

> You remember more if you take breaks every 10-20 minutes.

The main things which naturally help information move into long-term memory are: emotional impact, repetition and urgent need. The principles you can use to help you memorise things are:

imagination Make mental pictures

association Find as many links with other things as you can

exaggeration Make things bigger, brighter, louder

absurdity Imagine ridiculous associations

humour Make things funny

colour Try colour-coding associated items and ideas

sensuality Involve as many senses as possible

sexuality We remember things connected with sex

movement Link items to movements, gestures and facial expressions

order and sequence Things are easier to remember if they are ordered or sequenced (just putting items and objects into categories can be enough to remember them)

songs, rhymes, jingles and raps These are natural memory enhancers

REVIEW PERIODS

The most effective review periods to ensure things are retainted are after 10 minutes, 1 day, 1 week, 1 month and 6 months.

MNEMONICS

PIE.

I wish I could determine pi

'Eureka', cried the great inventor

Christmas pudding, Christmas pie

Is the problem's very centre

Count the letters in each word to give the value of pi: 3.14159265358979323846

MORE TO EXPLORE

Karen MARKOWITZ, Eric JENSEN **The Great Memory Book** The Brain Store 1999

Tony BUZAN **Use Your Memory** BBC 1984

Alan Baddeley **Your Memory – a user's guide** Prion 1996

Jo IDDON, Huw WILLIAMS **Memory Booster Workout** Hamlyn 2003

The Heart

We've known for a long time that the heart was the seat of our emotions – just look at all the expressions in English, and other languages, connecting the heart with feelings. (How many expressions contain the word 'heart'? What do almost all of them have in common?) Research has now proved it. The energy field of the heart is 150 times stronger than that of the brain and when a group of strangers meet together, their heart energy will be synchronised long before their brain energy.

learning by heart

Nor is the heart dependent on the brain – it is the other way round. There is more neural information going from the heart to the brain than from the brain to the heart, and according to Andrew Armour, an early pioneer in neuro-cardiology, the heart's nervous system qualifies as a 'brain'. Its network of neurons, neurotransmittors, proteins and support cells allows it to act independently of the brain. The heart is also a hormonal gland which releases two major hormones:

> *We know the truth not only by reason, but also by the heart.*
> **BLAISE PASCAL**

- ANF (Atrial Natriuretic Factor) which affects many of the body's major organs, including the regions of the brain that regulate our emotional state and influence learning and memory
- ICA (Intrinsic Cardiac Adrenergic) which synthesises and releases adrenalin and dopamine

In short, there is now proof that our emotions strongly influence our cognitive thinking, so it really is time to pay attention to emotional competence.

Look out for new information as it breaks, and meanwhile look for opportunities to increase emotional intelligence in teaching and training. *The HeartMath Solution* gives practical strategies, or you might consider doing a 'HeartMap' of what you feel instead of a mind map of what you think – follow the FREEZE-FRAME directions and when you reach step five, draw a representation of what you feel.

with all my heart

THE FIVE STEPS OF FREEZE-FRAME

A way to relieve stress, control emotions and attain a positive state for learning.

1 Recognise the stressful feeling and FREEZE-FRAME it. Take time out.
2 Shift your focus away from your racing mind to the area around your heart. Pretend you're breathing through your heart to focus your energy in this area for 10 seconds or more.
3 Recall and re-experience a positive, fun feeling or time you've had in life.
4 Using your intuition, common sense and sincerity, ask your heart *'What would be a more efficient response to the situation, one that would minimise future stress?'*
5 Listen to your heart's answer.

Adapted from **The HeartMath Solution**

> *Here is my secret, a very simple secret: it is only with the heart that one can see rightly; what is essential is invisible to the eye.*
> **ANTOINE DE SAINT-EXUPÉRY**

MORE TO EXPLORE

Carla HANNAFORD **Awakening the Child Heart** Jamilla Nur Publishing 2002. *A combination of science and real experience which gives the implications of the new understanding of the heart.*

Doc CHILDRE, Howard MARTIN **The HeartMath® Solution – proven techniques for developing Emotional Intelligence** Piatkus 1999. *Full details of the 'freeze-frame' technique and the proof that it works.*

Paul PEARSALL **The Heart's Code** Thorsons 1998. *Evidence from heart transplant patients that memories are also stored in the heart.*

www.heartmathsolution.com

Stress

Much has been written about the negative effects of stress and tension on the brain, on the person and on learning. Of course some stress can have a positive effect – without any physical tension we would all flop about like jellyfish, and without any mental tension we'd be unlikely to get anything done. So the question is the degree of stress.

Under too much stress, the body responds with an 'F***' response: Fight, Flight, Freeze or Flock. In the modern world, this translates as responding aggressively, running away, becoming tongue-tied, or ganging up with our friends. Do you recognise any teenagers of your aquaintance? Of course the dangerous effects of stress come from the chemicals which are all too easily released into our bloodstream but can take a long time to disperse. Too much stress, without enough recovery time, leads to negative effects on our health and our learning. The alternative, positive response to the right amount of stress is 'Flow' – that feeling of being on a high as you work in a relaxed productive way and accomplish an enormous amount of work apparently without effort. Isn't this the best way to learn?

The state of flow is characterised by 'relaxed alertness' – a state which can be achieved by meditation (page 39) or by many of the eastern practices such as Yoga, Tai Chi, Qi Gong, etc. There is much to be said simply for sitting up straight, taking a deep breath and sitting quietly for a few moments at the beginning of any period of study.

		BRAIN WAVES		
ᴡᴡᴡᴡ	**Beta**	β 13-25CPS	Conscious awareness. Logical thought, analysis. Wide awake, alert. Talking and doing.
ᴡᴡᴡᴡ	**Alpha**	α 8-12CPS	Relaxation and meditation. Daydreaming. Relaxed alertness that facilitates imagination, inspiration and fast assimilation of facts.
ᴡᴡᴡᴡ	**Theta**	θ 4-7CPS	Deep meditation, hypnosis. High suggestibility.
ᴡᴡᴡᴡ	**Delta**	δ 0.5-3CPS	Deep dreamless sleep.

CPS= cycles per second

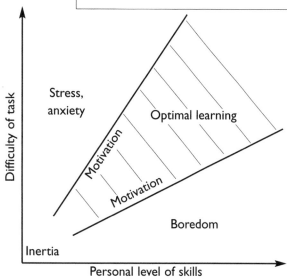

MORE TO EXPLORE

Sharon PROMISLOW **Putting Out the Fire of Fear: Extinguish the burning issues in your life** Enhanced learning 2002. *Counteracting stress and achieving optimal learning states through exercises, kinesiology and aspects of NLP.*

Herbert BENSON **The Relaxation Response** Collins 1975. *One of the first books to prove the benefits of relaxation and meditation.*

Meditation

Meditation is simply a case of relaxing the mind. It has similar benefits to relaxing the body: it counteracts stress, increases concentration and generally feels good. Why do it? Because it's one way of accessing your emotions, of getting into a good learning state (or simply a good state) at will, and a first step towards spiritual intelligence (page 32). The relaxed state of mind characterised by alpha brain waves (page 38) is generally considered the ideal state for learning and for creative thought.

The following 'meditations' can take less than a minute, although building up through three minutes to five and then more will bring greater benefits. Experiment with some of the following. Do not 'try' to achieve any particular state, just relax and do the 'activities'. There are no rules about how often you do it. Little and often is good, and the more you do it, the better you – and your students – will feel. With students, it is a good way to start the day, or the lesson, and as students get more experienced, they find it a useful way to calm themselves before an exam.

RELAX FROM TOP TO TOE

Starting Sit well, ie sit up straight with both feet on the floor, legs slightly apart, hands resting on your lap. Feel your head balanced on the top of your spine. Move it gently around till it is upright with your chin level with the floor. Close your eyes (or half close your eyes) if that feels comfortable.

Take a deep breath in through your nose and as you breathe out (through your nose) relax from the top of your head down to your feet – head, face, neck, shoulders, arms, hands, fingers, chest, back, stomach, backside, thighs, calves, ankles, feet, toes. Do it twice more. Enjoy the stillness.

Ending End any meditation gently, eg by rubbing your hands together, taking a deep breath in, covering your eyes with your hands and opening your eyes under your hands as you breathe out. Take your hands down – and make sure you wake up fully before you drive a car or use machinery.

COUNTING BREATHS

Sit well. Concentrate on your breathing. Do not breathe in any particular way. Just notice the temperature of the air as it comes in, and any slight change in its quality as you breathe out. After a moment, start counting your breaths. Use whatever counting system works for you (eg one in, two out; one in-out, two in-out).

COLOUR GAZING

Place a brightly coloured post-it note at one end of a blank white sheet of paper. Gaze at it unblinkingly for about a minute. Then cover it with your hand and transfer your gaze to the remaining space on the white paper. Wait a moment for the after image to appear. If it doesn't work the first time, try again with a different colour. Notice the different effects and after images you get with different colours. (This is a good first meditation for children.)

GAZING MEDITATION

Sit well and focus your gaze on one point straight ahead of you. Just notice what you can see – the colours, the shapes, what you are aware of in your peripheral vision. Keep your eyes relaxed. Blink if you need to. After a while, close your eyes and continue to notice what you can see internally – the after image, the colours inside your eyelids, etc. You can also gaze at a candle, a beautiful flower, a tree, a fire, the clouds, a mandala.

SENSES MEDITATION

Sit well. Keeping your head still, pay attention to everything you can see around you in your peripheral vision. Then still noticing what you can see, notice everything you can hear. Then add what you can feel. Rub your hands gently on your thighs and notice the sensation. Notice any smells. Take deeper breaths as you do so. And taste any tastes in you mouth. Be fully alive to the world of your senses. (You can do this one while walking too.)

MORE TO EXPLORE

David HARP **The New Three Minute Meditator** New Harbinger Publications Inc 1990

Peter RUSSELL **The TM Technique** Peter Russell 2000

Daniel GOLEMAN **The Meditative Mind** Crucible 1988

Self-Esteem

Our self-esteem and how we feel about ourselves has a huge impact, if not the greatest impact, on how we learn.

Self-esteem is more than just feeling good. It is about knowing and accepting who we are, and taking responsibility for our actions with a sense of personal integrity. It is about being able to function confidently in relation to other people.

This 'feeling' needs to be based on reality. Nathaniel Branden's definition of 'fully realised' self-esteem is *'the experience that we are appropriate to life and to the requirements of life'*. More specifically, self-esteem is confidence in

1 our ability to think and our ability to cope with the basic challenges of life; and
2 our right to be happy and successful, the feeling of being worthy, deserving, entitled to assert our needs and wants, achieve our values, and enjoy the fruits of our efforts.

> **BRANDEN'S SIX PILLARS**
> Living Consciously
> Self-Acceptance
> Self-Responsibility
> Self-Assertiveness
> Living Purposefully
> Personal Integrity

Robert Reasoner, President of the International Council for Self-Esteem, has developed a program called Building Self-Esteem, which has been used in schools in the USA for 25 years. It is designed to foster five elements:

1 **A sense of security** – by treating chidren with respect, letting them know what is expected of them, having clear rules which are upheld without intimidating or degrading them.
2 **A sense of identity** – by accepting children for who they are and breaking the vicious circle of 'I'm not loved so I'll beat them to it and prove that I'm not lovable, but it's my choice'.
3 **A sense of belonging** – by providing opportunities to learn social skills and work co-operatively with others.
4 **A sense of purpose** – by helping young people create visions of what they want to achieve and what kind of person they want to be.
5 **A sense of personal competence** – by offering options and possible ways to achieve goals, and give access to resources.

It should go without saying that those who are responsible for fostering the self-esteem of others will only be able to do so if they are confident of their own worth. The place to start is always with oneself.

> *A disservice is done to people if they are offered 'feel good' notions of self-esteem that divorce it from questions of consciousness, responsibility and moral choice.*
>
> **NATHANIEL BRANDEN**

MORE TO EXPLORE

Nathaniel BRANDEN **The Six Pillars of Self-Esteem** Bantam 1994. *The classic and best overview of what self-esteem is about.*

Eva HOFFMAN **For you dear teacher** Learn to Learn 2002. *A book which values teachers and gives practical suggestions to help them value themselves.*

Eva HOFFMAN **The Learning Adventure** Learn to Learn 2002. *Self-esteem and more for young children.*

The Self-Esteem Directory – *available only through SEAL*

www.circle-time.co.uk *Using circle time to enhance self-esteem.*

www.self-esteem-international.org *International Council for Self-Esteem*

Esteem1@aol.com *Self-Esteem Resources – for Reasoner's program*

Learning Environment

What message does your teaching room give to learners when they come in? Is it a pleasant, clean, practical and inspiring place to learn? Does it say to your students, 'You are worthy of pleasant surroundings', 'You are worth making an effort for'?

If it falls short in any way, what other learning environments can you think of that, in an ideal world, you would use as a model? Given that there are almost certainly constraints on the changes you can make, there are nonetheless things that all of us can do personally to improve the physical environment, both within our own teaching room and in the wider environment.

> *If you change the environment, you change the people.*
>
> BUCKMINSTER FULLER

The mind map below might give you some initial thoughts. But as it also shows, the physical environment is less than half the story. The emotional environment is even more important – and the teacher's role is crucial, as it is the teacher who sets the tone for all interactions and relationships in the classroom.

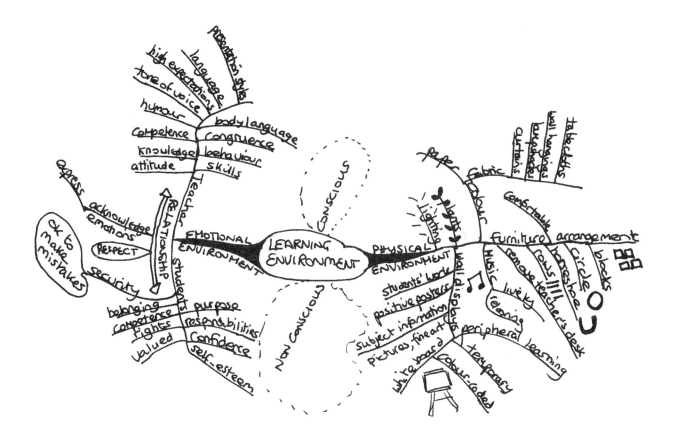

MORE TO EXPLORE

www.ltl.org.uk Learning Through Landscapes
www.hse.org.uk Human Scale Education

Music

Hearing is the first of the senses to develop after conception and the last to go when we are dying. The apparatus connected with hearing also has a profound effect on our ability to orientate ourselves, balance and move as well as communicate. Damage is done to this apparatus by overloud, heavy beat music. Conversely, in broad terms, 18-19th century classical music can enhance the functioning of the organism as a whole. Music involves many different aspects – timing, rhythm, tune, tone, volume, variety of instruments, type, etc – and the combinations give rise to almost infinite diversity and the benefits are myriad. There is also now scientific proof of the effect of music on the emotions.

In Lozanov's suggestopedia (page 45), music is a crucial component – using dramatic classical music for the 'active concerts' and more relaxing, particularly Baroque, music for the 'passive concerts'. Modern day Accelerated Learning tends to be more eclectic in its use of music – but if you want to get started, the best thing to do is experiment. What music might you use in the following situations?
- to welcome learners into the classroom
- to enliven learners when they're a bit sluggish, possibly during a stretch break
- to help relax learners, or during guided visualisations
- as background while learners are working individually or in groups
- setting the mood for particular sorts of lessons, themes or topics
- signalling a change
- fun music/sounds to introduce specific activities, eg a quick runaround activity, celebrating success
- going out with a bang – inspiring music to leave the room to

Music with words is fine for setting a mood while people are coming in or leaving, or if the words are specifically relevant to the setting up of an activity, but while people are thinking or working, music without words is less intrusive. Similarly, 'new age' music which doesn't have a specific 'tune' to latch on to is easier to study to than music with a strong beat, rhythm or tune, and harmonious classical music is generally more conducive to learning than modern popular music – unless you are using it for a specific purpose. And don't forget the power of silence. Music is played everywhere these days, to the point where it has become 'muzac', so it has much more power if used selectively.

KODÁLY

Those interested in teaching music per se might investigate the method of the Hungarian composer Zoltán Kodály (1882-1967), which starts with practical experience and traditional folk music. His message is of interest to all educators, and especially to those incorporating music into their teaching of other subjects.

There is a map of the emotions, the mind – even the soul?

It is music.
We may not have learnt how to read the map yet, but it is there.

PAUL ROBERTSON

Music is an indispensible part of universal human knowledge.

ZOLTÁN KODÁLY

Mozart Effect

The term 'Mozart Effect' is used in many ways, from specific scientific terminology to an all-embracing term covering any effect produced by any piece of music.

Wolfgang Amadeus Mozart (1756 – 1791) was a musical genius, child prodigy and one of the most prolific composers ever known. His music comes at a cusp in the development of Western classical music – linking the regular and repetitive music of the Baroque (eg Vivaldi, Bach) to the increasingly emotional and explosive Classical and Romantic period (eg Schubert, Beethoven). He wrote 627 known works in a delightful and unmistakable style.

Mozart's music has been used for decades in music therapy by innovators such as Alfred Tomatis (1920 – 2001). Tomatis' hypothesised that 'good learners are good listeners'. His method involves listening to Mozart through an 'electronic ear', a device which can be set to filter out sounds of a given frequency, to train the ear to listen more fully. This led to successes in treating ADHD, autism and dyslexia. Tomatis experimented with many composers but always found

Mozart most effective. He wrote a book on this mystery, 'Pourquoi Mozart?'

The term 'Mozart Effect' was first used in describing a series of experiments by researchers at the University of California, Irvine. Undergraduates preparing for a spatio-temporal IQ test (pattern-analysis, multiple choice matrices and paper figure visualisation tests) by listening to 10 minutes of Mozart's Sonata for Two Pianos (K448) scored 8-9 points higher than those listening to silence or a spoken relaxation tape. This improvement was not accompanied by an increase in pulse rate, ruling out simple physiological effects. Further experiments compared Mozart to Philip Glass, dance music and a story, with the same results. However, the improvement was not permanent – it faded after about 10 minutes.

The Irvine group, led by Gordon Shaw and Frances Rauscher, continued to investigate this 'Mozart Effect' with further experiments, including the effect of piano keyboard lessons on pre-school children (again boosting spatio-temporal ability, but this time not fading out so quickly).

Other researchers attempted to replicate the initial findings, with mixed success – in some cases these were simply due to failing to accurately replicate the experiment. Yet others refuse to accept the results as being anything other than a simple excitement factor, despite this being explicitly ruled out in the initial experiments.

However, there is plenty of evidence that music (in general, not just Mozart) affects the mind and body. It is used in all cultures for many purposes including ritual, healing, community, family, entertainment and relaxation. This more general use of music to positively affect mind, body and mood is an exciting area. Musician and healer Don Campbell has produced a series of books and CDs under the Mozart Effect name which present a whole range of evidence and possibilities for using music in our everyday lives. And again Mozart can be found to lead the way. Campbell ascribes this to the fact that compared to other composers Mozart is often rated by listeners as relatively emotionally neutral.

The research goes on.

Contributed by Mark McKergow

HINT If you are switching off music before it reaches the end, turn the volume down gradually so you don't destroy the mood you have been creating. It can be less intrusive to 'fade in' music too. If you are using background music during an activity, turning it up quite loud before you turn it off can be an effective way of alerting people to the end of the activity.

COPYRIGHT Remember that there can be copyright considerations when playing music publicly. Check carefully. If possible buy or get someone to devise and record royalty-free music.

SINGING

Singing brings special benefits. Quite apart from the ease with which words can be remembered when set to music, choirboys at choir schools have been shown to have a higher reading age and higher IQ, due to their study of music (the specialised 'language' of musical notation, Latin, timing, etc), the multi-task activity of singing while reading notes and words, and the physical effects of singing (effect on breathing, listening, lung capacity, vocal equipment). And it makes people feel good too – the effect brought about by the change in gases in the blood acts as a natural mood enhancer. Quite apart from being a natural memory aid (it's much easier to remember the words of songs than straight text), and bringing all the individual positive benefits, singing is also a wonderful group activity. It literally brings us into harmony with ourselves and with one another.

Variations on singing, such as toning and chanting, have similar physical effects and also bring the added benefits of meditation (page 39).

TONING

A toning exercise to set you up for the day:

Stand upright, legs slightly apart, shoulders and abdomen relaxed. Take a deep breath in and on the outbreath make the sound 'ah' on any note you choose. Keep it going as long as you comfortably can as loudly as you comfortably can, keeping your throat open and relaxed.

From Healing with the Voice

Do it again several times choosing different notes each time. Some will be clearer and easier than others. After about eight different notes, choose the one which feels most comfortable, and tone it joyfully.

You can also exercise your facial muscles by saying the five vowel sounds on each note: *ay, eee, eye, oh, ooo.*

MORE TO EXPLORE

Gordon L SHAW **Keeping Mozart in Mind** Academic Press 1999. *The original 'Mozart Effect' research presently clearly if rather academically. Not an easy read.*

Elizabeth MILES **Tune Your Brain** Berkeley Publishing Group 1997. *A comprehensive and well-researched guide to how music influences mind, body and mood.*

Don CAMPBELL **The Mozart Effect** Hodder and Stoughton 2002 (revised edition). *Collection of tales, research and experiences about Mozart, music and mind.*

Lenn MILLBLOWER **Training with a beat – the teaching power of music** Stylus 2000. *Overview of music and its use in teaching/training – plus list of (mainly popular) music.*

Chris BREWER **Music & Learning – seven ways to use music in the classroom** LifeSounds 1995. *Overview of how to use music – with many classical music suggestions.*

James D'ANGELO **Healing with the Voice** Thorsons 2000. *Exercises from many disciplines to develop the voice.*

www.mozarteffect.com *Don Campbell's website with information, activities and suggestions.*

www.thepowerofmusic.co.uk *Susan Hallam of the Institute of Education, London – lots of information about music and its effects.*

www.mindinst.org *The original Mozart Effect researchers run the Music Intelligence Neural Development Institute, with resources for parents, educators and researchers.*

www.musicbakery.com *Source of high-quality thematic royalty-free music.*

Email Lenn Millblower and ask to receive his regular tips on using music in training: lennmillbower@offbeattraining.com

See also **Sound Healing** (page 50)

Suggestopedia

Suggestopedia is the learning system devised by Georgi Lozanov, the Bulgarian psychologist (born 1926) who started working on his method in the 1960s. It was developed as a language learning method, although it can be applied to learning anything. His work is better known in the west by its derivative, Accelerated Learning (page 9), although not everything that calls itself AL is suggestopedic. There is much about suggestopedia which is crucial to the understanding and practice of learning, in particular the importance of non-conscious learning (page 22). It is a sobering thought that after all this time Lozanov's important insights and understandings are still not accepted, or mostly even known about, in mainstream education.

Lozanov underwent 'trial by media' in the west in the 1980s when his work was misrepresented as being based on hypnosis – and therefore 'bad' – possibly because of the misunderstanding of the name 'suggestopedia'. Although some of his early research as a psychiatrist was on hypnosis as a way of controlling pain therapeutically, he insists that it plays no part in his teaching method. Suggestopedia accesses the massive learning potential of the non-conscious mind, but it is not necessary to put students into a trance to do so.

A SUGGESTOPEDIC COURSE

A course is typically four weeks long for six hours per day for 12 students with one teacher. The specific stages of each lesson (which is spread over three days – one afternoon, the next day and the following morning) are:

- **Introduction** Setting the scene through drama, realia, humour, etc.
- **Active Concert** A suggestopedic text (see next page) is read dramatically to music while students listen and follow the written version.
- **Passive Concert** Learners sit back and relax as they listen to the teacher reading the text at normal speed and without any distortion to a background of gentle baroque music.
- **Elaboration** All the practice activities which are familiar to most communicative language teachers: songs, rhymes, games, repetition, dialogues, etc.

Most articles about suggestopedia concentrate on the concert readings (since they are the part which is unique to the method). In fact about 75% of class time is spent on the elaboration section – the practical 'activation' section.

Although many AL practitioners often use the second, passive concert reading as a revision and consolidation at the end of the day, or first thing the following day, Lozanov did both concert readings together, viewing them both as initial input sessions.

> *Suggestopedia relies on success – that's what gives the joy.*
> **GEORGI LOZANOV**

Georgi Lozanov, founder of suggestopedia, in Uppsala, Sweden in 2002

Photo: Hugh L'Estrange

KEY ELEMENTS

- **Suggestopedic Text**

    The text is much longer than one would normally expect in a language class and much less simplified, which raises the expectation that learners can learn this much with ease. It is written in the target language down one side of the page, with the translation into the students' native language alongside (so students are confident that they can understand at all stages). In 'pure' suggestopedic lessons, the text is a 'play' divided into a number of 'acts' – each act being the focus of one 'lesson'.

- **Learning environment**

    The external environment of the classroom is made as attractive and comfortable as possible, with posters and pictures on the walls giving subliminal messages about the target language or the material to be learnt. The environment should also be safe and secure so that the learners' internal environment – how they feel about themselves, the subject, the teacher, the method, etc – is catered for. The emphasis on the arts – visual, poetic, dramatic and musical – raises an expectation of quality.

- **Teacher authority**

    'Teacher authority' is not about the teacher being authoritarian. The teacher should be seen as a figure in whom learners have confidence, someone they can trust and respect and who respects and has high expectations of them.

- **Student empowerment**

    The atmosphere set up by the teacher is specifically designed to empower students to express themselves freely and take responsibility for their own learning within a secure framework.

Teaching the first suggestopedic play, *Dr Aybolit*, in Sofia, Bulgaria

---

THE SUGGESTION

Lozanov chose the name 'suggestopedia 'because he wanted to suggest to the learner that learning is easy and quick. He later went through a phase of calling the method 'Desuggestopedia' since he realised that he had to 'desuggest' the usual expectation (or suggestion) in most learners' minds that learning is difficult and slow.

He claimed that most language courses imply this because they break the language down into such small chunks which have to be practised over and over again before the learner can move on to the next similarly predigested small chunk of language.

His own method, in contrast, gives exposure to large enough chunks of real unsimplified language for the non-conscious mind to begin to make its own sense of it.

BARRIERS TO LEARNING

Lozanov identified three barriers to learning:

- **Critical-logical** We reject things which don't seem sensible
- **Intuitive-affective** We reject things which harm us emotionally
- **Ethical** We reject beliefs which do not coincide with our own

SUGGESTION-DESUGGESTION

The means of the suggestive-desuggestive process listed by Lozanov are:

- **Complete competence** The 'authority' of the teacher
- **Infantilisation** Having the openness to learning of a child
- **Double-planeness** As well as learning the direct content of the lesson consciously, students are also being influenced non-consciously, at a subtle level, by the way the method is implemented
- **Concert, intonation, pseudo-passiveness and rhythm** The way the text is read to music during the concert readings, with special emphasis on the intonation and rhythm, is designed to induce a relaxed state in learners (the concert pseudo-passiveness), an optimal state for learning.

Lozanov made great claims for the success of his method, based on the 'scientific' fact that students could remember much more vocabulary than with other methods. Although this is true, whether or not the method is truly 'scientific' has been questioned, particularly as Lozanov uses the science to insist that it cannot be adapted in any way. In practice, most 'suggestopedic' teachers have incorporated aspects of language learning which were unknown at the time Lozanov first proposed (and researched) his method, but the fact that they still wish to call themselves suggestopedic teachers shows the huge debt they all feel to the originator and to the method, which clearly has much to offer teachers and learners.

Photo: Susan Norman

Lozanov in Venice in 1999

Georgi Lozanov with Evelyna Gateva, his partner in life and learning

Photo: Grethe Hooper Hansen

WHAT'S IN A NAME?

Suggestology is the theoretical understanding proposed by Lozanov. **Suggestopedia** is the teaching method based on the theory. Most people agree that the name does the method no favours. Nor do the names **Desuggestology/ Desuggestopedia** or **ReCaCo** (Reserve Capacity Communication) – both of which Lozanov used for a short time.

It became known as **Accelerated** (or **Accelerative) Learning**, then **Superlearning** (after the book of that title), **Intensive Learning** (in Russia) – and many other methods based on suggestopedia go by various other names.

MORE TO EXPLORE

Georgi Lozanov **Suggestology and Outlines of Suggestopedia** Gordon & Breach Pub 1978. *A fascinating but not particularly readable account from the man himself.*

Georgi LOZANOV, Evalina GATEVA **The Foreign Language Teacher's Suggestopedic Manual** Gordon & Breach Pub 1981. *Detailed information about suggestopedic language courses.*

Sheila OSTRANDER, Lynn SCHROEDER **Superlearning** Sphere Books 1979; updated as **Superlearning 2000** Souvenir Press 1996. *The book that drew the western world's attention to Lozanov's work.*

Charlotte LeHECKA **Historical Review of Accelerated Learning** International Alliance for Learning (IAL) 2003. *Excellent summary of the development of AL and Suggestopedia.*

See also bibliography for **Accelerated Learning** (page 13)

There's more to learning ...

The first part of this book has included information which most AL practitioners would agree is of direct relevance to Accelerated Learning today. The second part of this book looks at other systems and approaches in which SEAL members are involved. Although SEAL's original purpose was to promote the work of Georgi Lozanov, the founders, Michael Lawlor and Peter O'Connell, had the foresight to allow for the probability that new ideas would be developed and included in SEAL's remit. The subject matter of the second part of the book, therefore, gives access to some other ideas which have been the way into SEAL for many members.

The selection is personal and eclectic. It would be impossible to include everything. The fact that something is included here does not necessarily mean that all SEAL members subscribe to the ideas. However, they are all relevant to the larger questions to do with whole-person learning and personal and professional transformation. The richness of SEAL comes from the cross-fertilisation of ideas, and the more we learn, the more we discover that they are all inter-related. There is no way to do justice to them all, so we start with a mention of some which do not even have a page to themselves, with information about where to find more.

APPRECIATIVE INQUIRY

David Cooperrider was the originator of this change management tool to enhance productivity. It aims to replace negativity, criticism and diagnosis with discovery, dream and design. It looks for and builds on what is best in people, organisations and the world, by asking positive key questions. The premise is that we have choice.

David L COOPERRIDER et al **The Appreciative Inquiry Handbook**

www.appreciative-inquiry.org

AUTOGENIC TRAINING

Autogenic Training, meaning 'self-regulation', was developed around 1932 by Johannes Schultz. It is based on autohypnosis and the notion that the mind can influence the body and balance the systems that control 'involuntary' actions such as breathing, circulation, heart rate, etc. Its immediate benefits are reduction in the negative effects of stress, and it is also a very effective holistic therapy.

Kai KERMANI **Autogenic Training: The Effective Holistic Way to Better Health** 1996

www.autogenic-therapy.org.uk

CONSTELLATIONS

Similar to psychodrama, constellations is a group dynamic process whereby the issues of an individual or group are examined by others playing out significant roles in the 'drama'.

Ursula FRANKE **The River Never Looks Back: historical and practical foundations of Bert Hellinger's family constellations** 2003

www.hellinger.com

www.nadt.org

DRAMA IN EDUCATION (DIE)

Using drama as a teaching method rather than as a performance. The process is more important than the product and the participants learn through being involved physically and emotionally with the action.

Betty Jane WAGNER **Dorothy Heathcote: drama as a learning medium** 1999

www.nationaldrama.co.uk *National Association for Teachers of Drama (NATD)*

EASTERN PHILOSOPHIES

Although subjects such as **Yoga, Tai Chi** and **Qi Gong** are often treated as gentle alternatives to exercise in the west, they are all based on profound and ancient philosophies to do with the nature of the universe and our role in it. Western science is now taking more of an interest in these philosophies which have many correlations with the quantum view of the universe (page 79).

Many holistic therapies are base on similar understandings. Without wanting here to recommend anything in particular, this is cerrtainly an area of fascinating exploration for anyone interested in holistic teaching and learning. The body, exercise, physical therapies such as the Alexander Technique, massage, etc, and nutrition might all feature at a SEAL conference.

The web or any bookstore will be a rich source of information.

KINESIOLOGY

Kinesiology means 'science of movement'. Applied Kinesiology, AK was founded in 1964 by the American chiropractor, George Goodheart, who discovered that normal and abnormal body functions could be diagnosed by 'muscle testing' – using the innate wisdom of the body by asking questions to determine what makes a muscle strong and what weakens it. It has developed in many different directions and most teachers come to it through 'Touch for Health' or Educational Kinesiology, also known as Brain Gym (page 20).

Maggie LA TOURELLE, Anthea COURTENAY **Principles of Kinesiology** HarperCollins 1997

John F THIE **Touch for Health** DeVorss & Co 1979

Charles KREBS **A Revolutionary Way of Thinking** Hill of Content 1998

www.kinesiology.net

www.touch4health.com

PSYCHODRAMA

Conceived by Jacob Moreno, psyschodrama uses structured drama to examine, clarify and hopefully resolve problems and issues raised by an individual. (Sociodrama works in the same way in relation to groups.) The **protagonist** is the person (or persons) selected to represent the theme of the group. Other group members assuming roles in the drama are called **auxiliary egos**. Group members who watch are the **audience**, representing the world at large. The **stage** is the physical space in which the action occurs. The **director** is the trained psychodramatist who guides participants through the session.

www.psychodrama.org

Bernard DUFEU **Teaching Myself** Oxford University Press 1994. *Psychodrama applied to foreign language teaching.*

PSYCHOSYNTHESIS

by Grethe Hooper Hansen

Psychosynthesis is a humanistic psychology created by Roberto Assagioli (1888-1974) in Italy. The goal is the realisation of individual potential through the acceptance and harmonisation of all the different elements of our personality: body, mind, feelings and spirit. Normally, since human beings have both a light and shadow side, we reject and deny those elements we regard as negative, seeing them only by projection in people other than ourselves. Assagioli made an immense contribution to psychotherapy through the techniques he created, many of which were adapted from eastern mysticism. He is particularly known for the introduction of visualisation or guided imagery, and his perception that the greater the sensory and emotional involvement, the more effective the results will be – by harnessing the motor, autonomic and unconscious intelligence of the body/mind. His work anticipates the 'organic' approach of the 21st century.

Roberto ASSAGIOLI **Psychosynthesis** Turnstone 1980 (originally 1965)

Piero FERRUCCI **What We May Be** Turnstone 1983

Diana WHITMORE **Psychosynthesis, Counselling in Action** Sage Publications 1999 (orig 1991)

www.psychosynthesis.edu

PERSONAL DEVELOPMENT COURSES

There are several organisations which provide short courses for personal development. Participants examine their existing beliefs and 'stories', and how these have come about; they then explore the true nature of possibility, choice and transformation and what holds us back (fear, the past).

www.landmarkeducation.com *The Landmark Forum*

www.higherawareness.com *Insight*

www.talentfoundation.org *The Talent Foundation*

TETRAMAP®

The TetraMap is a model developed by Yoshimi and Jon Brett that maps the complexity of nature into the four basic elements: Earth, Air, Water and Fire. Then, using the power of metaphor, the map is applied to human behaviour to give insights into personality, team building, styles of leadership, organisational development, creativity, future planning, and finding sustainable peaceful solutions. So far it has mainly been applied in business.

Yoshimi & Jon Brett **TetraMap – how to develop people and business the way nature intended** A Learnology Publication 2002

www.tetramap.com

Learning Difficulties

Dyslexia, dyspraxia, ADHD – there are many different conditions which make learning difficult and probably as many causes as there are individuals with those difficulties. In fact many of the approaches mentioned elsewhere in this book were developed to help overcome learning difficulties, but the following are additional possible sources of information.

DYSLEXIA

This term in the UK is used broadly to cover a range of learning difficulties. In the US, it is used more specifically to refer to problems with the written word. (Dyspraxia refers to problems with physical manipulation.) Many dyslexics see themselves as privileged, after all it didn't hold back people such as Leonardo da Vinci, the statesman Winston Churchill or the entrepreneur Richard Branson.

Diane BARTLETT, Sylvia MOODY **Dyslexia in the Workplace** Garnder's 2000.

www.hornsby.co.uk *Hornsby International Dyslexia Centre*

INSTRUMENTAL ENRICHMENT

Instrumental Enrichment (IE) and Mediated Learning Experience (MLE) are based on the work of Israeli psychologist Reuven Feuerstein who developed his theory in the late 40s through his work with children who were orphaned or separated from their parents as a result of the Holocaust. An intervention program, it is based on the belief that intelligence is modifiable and not fixed, and it is designed to enhance the cognitive skills necessary for independent thinking. IE aims to sharpen critical thinking with the concepts, skills, strategies, operations and attitudes necessary for independent learning; to diagnose and correct deficiencies in thinking skills; and to help individuals 'learn to learn'.

Reuven FEUERSTEIN, Yacov RAND, John E RYNDERS **Don't accept me as I am; helping 'retarded' people to excel** Skylight Professional Development 1998

www.zipcon.net/~highroad/ie.htm

www.icelp.org *Feuerstein's own organisation*

LIGHT AND COLOUR THERAPIES

Relatively recently 'SAD' (Seasonal Affective Disorder) has come to the notice of the public. When people are deprived of natural light, they can display a variety of symptoms such as lethargy, anxiety, lack of concentration, interpersonal difficulties and depression. This often lifts of its own accord in spring when sufferers have access to more natural light – or through treatment with full-spectrum light. This is only one of the ways in which light and colour are being used to treat a variety of developmental and learning problems.

Jacob LIBERMAN et al **Light Years Ahead** Celestial Arts 1954. *A compendium of approaches using light.*

RETAINED REFLEXES

Babies are born with certain reflexes which are important for their development as babies, but which normally disappear of their own accord by the time the child is of school age. If they don't they can cause children enormous physical and learning difficulties which often go unrecognised.

Sally GODDARD **Reflexes, Learning and Behavior** Fern Ridge Press 2002. *A non-invasive approach to solving learning and behaviour problems.*

RIGHT-BRAIN APPROACHES

Many of the brain-friendly accelerated learning approaches in the first half of this book are more suitable for right brain learners than 'stand and deliver' information-transfer teaching.

Barbara MEISTER VITALE **Unicorns are real – a right-brain approach to learning** (1982) and **Free Flight – celebrating your right brain** (1986) Jalmar Press *Right-brain approaches from an extreme right-brainer and dyslexic.*

SOUND THERAPIES

Sound in the form of the human voice, instruments, music and directed frequencies have been shown to have beneficial effects on health and learning.

www.tomatis.com *The Tomatis Society*

Paul ROBERTSON **Music and the Mind** Channel 4 TV 1996. *Book and video of the TV series looking at links between the workings of the brain, music, emotions and learning disorders.*

The Listening Program Advanced Brain Technologies 1999 www.advancedbrain.com *Listening programme developed from Tomatis' work – can be done unsupervised at home.*

Early Years

The answer to the nature/nurture question seems to be 'thirds': approximately one third of life's chances come from our genes, about one third from experience within the first five years of life, and the remaining third from further experiences throughout life. It therefore follows that the first five years of life – plus the crucial nine months in utero – are extremely important in terms of our learning and development. Some of the important work that's going on in this area is:

PRE-BIRTH

Mikhail Lazarev (pictured right) in Russia has developed the SONATAL method of teaching pregnant mothers to sing to the unborn child – plus a 'sounding belt' so that the foetus can kick back a response! The program continues after the child is born. A similar program has been developed in Croatia.

BIRTH

Michel Odent pioneered waterbirthing in the UK after working with Frederic Leboyer in France. His own work focuses on the crucial importance of the hormonal bonding period between mother and child immediately before and for about an hour after birth. He is bringing together research which proves the negative effects of not honouring this bonding process – from adolescent violence to increased tooth decay!

SIGN WITH YOUR BABY

Babies can learn to sign their needs and thoughts before they have developed the necessary aparatus to speak. Joseph Garcia developed one of the first systems to teach parents how to communicate with their children and teach the children to respond through signs. Children get less frustrated because they are able to communicate and their improved communication skills frequently lead to them speaking earlier.

Photos: Sign with your Baby

SMART

SMART (Stimulating Maturity through Accelerated Readiness Training) is a school-wide program developed by Lyelle Palmer which provides the necessary stimulation and preparation for the development of numeracy and literacy skills at pre-school and primary level. The emphasis is on nurturing the physical development which is necessary before children are ready to read and write: vestibular/balance development (eg through spinning, hanging upside down), gross motor movements, uni-lateral and bi-lateral co-ordination, fine motor movements, muscle strength and flexibility, etc.

MORE TO EXPLORE

Michel ODENT **The Scientification of Love** (1999) and **The Farmer and the Obstetrician** Free Association Books 2002

Alison GOPNIK, Andrew MELTZOFF, Patricia KUHL **How babies think** Phoenix 1999. *Readable research-based information about what babies know and how they know it.*

Marian DIAMOND, Janet HOPSON **Magic Trees of the Mind - how to nurture your child's intelligence, creativity and healthy emotions from birth through adolescence** Plume/Penguin 1998

Deborah JACKSON **Baby Wisdom** Hodder & Stoughton 2002. *Cross-cultural view of how people care for babies and young children.*

Contact details for everyone on this page from SEAL.

Alternative Schooling

T his is a thumbnail sketch of various schools and educational approaches for young learners which might serve as useful models for anyone looking for alternatives to mainstream education.

MONTESSORI

Developed by Maria Montessori (1870-1952), the method focuses totally on the developmental needs of the young child. Originally she developed apparatus for mental, sensory and physical stimulation for use with mentally retarded children, and she had such good results that she opened a 'Casa di Bambini' in 1907 in a slum district in Rome. She believed that children should develop self-esteem

through being responsible for themselves and their environment, that there should be no distinction between work and play and freedom within a well-prepared environment – where all children could be doing the activity they chose. She developed child-size furniture, dressing frames (to practise buttons, etc), sandpaper letters, colour tablets, smelling bottles, tasting jars … and many more practical learning aids which are still available and relevant today.

MORE TO EXPLORE

Lynne LAWRENCE **Montessori Read & Write** Three Rivers Press 1998. *Practical guide for parents (and teachers)*

The Montessori Foundation www.montessori.org

VYGOTSKY

Russian psychologist Lev Semyonovich Vygotsky (1896-1934) extended the idea of humans' use of tools to their use of 'tools for the mind' as a way of viewing mental development. Vygotsky thought the tools not only extended our natural abilities, they also change the way we pay attention, remember and think. The teacher's role is to 'arm children' with the mental tools they need to become active tool users and independent tool makers.

Vygotsky is also known for his belief that learning occurs in the area just beyond what we already know – the 'Zone of Proximal Development'. He defined the ZPD as 'the difference in the child's achievement in assisted versus unassisted performance'. Learning in the ZPD is associated with an interaction between spontaneous concepts of the child and systematic 'scientific' concepts introduced by the teacher'.

MORE TO EXPLORE

There is a need for a practical introduction to Vygotsky's ideas. Both books by Vygotsky himself are fascinating, but somewhat hard going.

Lev VYGOTSKY **Thought and Language** The MIT Press 1986

LS VYGOTSKY **Mind in Society: The Development of Higher Psychological Processes** Harvard University Press 1978

www.kolar.org/vygotsky

STEINER WALDORF

The philosopher and writer, Rudolf Steiner (1861-1925), set up the first school in Stuttgart in 1919 for the children of employees of the Waldorf-Astoria cigarette factory. Steiner Waldorf education represents the essential nature of childhood, enabling all children to develop their innate capacities and self-confidence in a caring, child-sensitive environment. At pre-school and primary stages, children are given a foundation for emotional and cognitive intelligence, a sense of values and responsibility, creativity and initiative. Children's natural enthusiasm and wonder are encouraged as essential qualities for life-long learning. Pupils benefit greatly from the continuity of having the same teacher throughout their school life (kindergarten, class teacher for ages 6 to 14, self-chosen tutor and class guardian from 14 to 18). Teachers are free to choose and adapt material appropriate to individual situations and to shape and present it creatively. From the youngest classes up to school-leaving age, subjects are integrated thematically within a spiral curriculum which enhances students' understanding of complex interrelationships between different phenomena. The approach is possibly best known for incorporating the dance form 'eurythmy', and for their understanding of the importance of the use of art.

MORE TO EXPLORE

Lynne OLDFIELD **Free to Learn – Introducing Steiner Waldorf Early Childhood Education** Hawthorn Press 2001

Gilbert CHILDS **Rudolf Steiner: his Life and Work** Floris Books 1995

Gilbert CHILDS **Steiner Education** Floris Books 1995

All simple clear introductions to the man and the schools.

www.steinerwaldorf.org.uk

REGGIO EMILIA

The approach, named after the district in Italy where it was developed, is based on the premise that children have an incredible curiosity that makes them search for the reasons for everything. It was developed by parents who were so appalled by their own inability to stop the rise of Mussolini that they determined their children should be brought up to think independently. The system is based on projects proposed by the pre-school children for whom it is intended. The arts are given a high priority and there is a stringent documentation process which is a record of the process itself. It is made available to parents and teachers as a record of individual and group achievement as well as providing the basis for further teaching input.

> *'Reggio successfully challenges so many false dichotomies: art versus science, individual versus community, child versus adult, enjoyment versus study, nuclear family versus extended family. It does this by achieving a unique harmony that spans these contrasts. Reggio epitomizes for me an education that is effective and humane; its students undergo a sustained apprenticeship in humanity, one that may last a lifetime.'*
>
> Howard Gardner

MORE TO EXPLORE

C EDWARDS, L GANDINI, G FORMAN(Eds) **The Hundred Languages of Children: the Reggio Emilia Approach to Early Childhood** Education Ablex 1993

www.ericfacility.net/ericdigests/ed354988.html

IEDERWIJS

In The Netherlands, 'iederwijs' ('in your own way') is a growing organisation setting up independent alternative schooling based on Steiner, Montessori, Reggio ... and others. The focus is totally on the needs of the child, and learning occurs within the normal framework of child-chosen activities.

Thanks to Anne Mijke van Harten for the information in this section.

Photos supplied by Hanneke Beckers of Aventurijn

MORE TO EXPLORE

www.aventurijn.org
www.deregenboogbrug
www.jenaplan.nl

Humanistic Language Teaching

Suggestology and Accelerated Learning approaches were initially only applied to language learning, since learning a language has often been considered the 'ultimate' test while knowledge of new vocabulary is relatively easy to test 'scientifically'. There is certainly more AL material published in relation to language learning than any other subject. The following approaches, together with suggestopedia (page 45), are often grouped under the title 'humanistic'. The emphasis in all of them is that the teacher is the supportive, non-judgmental facilitator of learning who coaches learners to develop their own criteria and take the responsibility for their own learning.

MORE TO EXPLORE

Earl STEVICK **Humanism in language teaching** Oxford University Press 1990. *Good overview.*

Jane ARNOLD (Ed) **Affect in Language Learning** Cambridge University Press 1999. *Specialists introduce many ways to use affective factors to make language teaching and learning more effective.*

Accelerated Learning language courses (French, German, Italian, Spanish) Accelerated Learning Systems Ltd 1985

www.hltmag.co.uk *Website for language teachers by Pilgrims Language School, Canterbury*

COMMUNITY LANGUAGE LEARNING

Community Language Learning (CLL), also known as 'Counselling Learning', was created by Charles A Curran, a professor of psychology, and was developed by one of his students, Paul La Forge. It derives from the pioneering work of Carl Rogers, founder of person-centred therapy. Curran emphasised both the role of the learner as an individual and as a member of the group (known as the 'community'). Learners are referred to as 'clients', emphasising the importance of genuine human interaction in language learning, and the teacher assumes the role of 'counsellor', giving support, encouragement and advice – a very different role to that of a teacher imparting knowledge.

The method generally assumes a group of clients with the same mother tongue who usually sit in a circle with the counsellor on the outside. They whisper what they want to say to the counsellor (or another bilingual 'knower') who translates into the target language. The learner repeats this to other group members and/or tape-records it. Students repeat and record several translated sentences. This self-generated material can then be replayed and written up, and the counsellor can direct attention to specific aspects of the language within the tapescript. After the language learning activities, participants reflect on and share their feelings – a central part of the method as the process is a group interaction. There is no syllabus or curriculum as language derives totally from teacher-learner interaction.

STAGES OF LEARNING

identified by Charles Curran

1 **Birth** Students don't know the target language and are completely dependent on the teacher.
2 **Self** Students begin to use the new language with the aid of the teacher.
3 **Separate existence** Students use language independently of the teacher and may begin to resist teacher's intervention.
4 **Adolescence** Students are able to express themselves, but may be aware of gaps in their knowledge.
5 **Independence** Students can continue their learning without assistance. They may also act as counsellors to less advanced students.

MORE TO EXPLORE

Charles A CURRAN **Counseling-Learning in Second Languages** Apple River Press 1976. *A comprehensive treatment of the theory behind CLL.*

TOTAL PHYSICAL RESPONSE

Total Physical Response (TPR) is a way of using movement, gesture and group dynamics, linked with spoken language in the form of commands, to create an atmosphere in which learners quickly and easily acquire comprehension of new vocabulary and structures. In the process, something called 'impulse to language' comes into play.

It was from his observation of how babies learn their first language that James Asher gained the insights on which TPR is founded. Babies don't actually talk, but they do listen when they are spoken to, and they respond, typically with movement – a smile or a simple action. Asher refers to these exchanges as 'language-body conversations'. When the baby responds, she is rewarded with verbal petting. By the time children are two and a half, they are capable of understanding (but not speaking) long, grammatically-complex instructions such as '*Stop hitting your little sister and go and sit down and watch the television with Aunty Sue*'. No-one ever tries seriously to teach children to talk. They just start when they're ready. And typically parents don't bother correcting children's mistakes, because they know all will come right in the end. So without any teaching and with little or no overt correction of errors, this 'method' has a 100% success rate.

At the core of TPR lies the notion that humans are probably biologically hard-wired to acquire language by responding physically to language, and then internalising both vocabulary and grammar until they reach a stage when they are ready to start talking, a stage Asher calls 'comprehension literacy'. According to TPR theory, language acquisition is a linear progression: comprehension first, then speech. This notion is supported by the architecture of the brain, which appears to have two distinct regions, one dedicated to controlling speech (Broca's area) and one for comprehension of speech (Wernicke's area).

Photos: Robin Cain

A TPR classroom

This is not just a method for beginners. When the grammar starts to get tough, TPR comes into its own. With more advanced students, the room is fringed with realia – a kitchen, a shop, an office, a wild west saloon. If you're pushed for space, use minimal props and be creative. You still work with helpers. You start by modelling your own commands and getting the group to follow instructions, but because there is so much more language available, you can create a rich verbal environment. Complex grammar items are, after all, only notionally complex. Intellectually, people are capable of dealing with very complex ideas.

ARE YOU ALREADY DOING TPR?

Many teachers already incorporate aspects of 'physical response' in their teaching, but check your practice against this TPR list to see whether you're using the total model:

- You never, under any circumstances, try to 'catch out' a student who is performing commands. The performance is the learning process. Correcting mistakes too early changes a party into a nightmare.
- Language is not translated or explained. Students see, understand and act.
- Students are not asked to speak until they have chosen to start speaking. As their comprehension increases, their desire to speak will emerge. This may not happen for several lessons. When it does, you go with the flow. Until it does, you don't force it.
- Students are never isolated. They always work in pairs or groups until you're sure everyone knows exactly what to do. Only then do we ask students to perform alone.
- Bizarre and 'off the wall' commands are keys to memory. *'Touch your nose to the window'* is not only good theatre, it is also memorable language.

TPR LESSON SEQUENCE

- The teacher gives a command verbally and models it himself.
- He asks two helpers to model it with him while the others watch.
- He asks the whole class to follow his command.
- He asks groups within the class to model the command.

Then after some sessions, when the students express the desire to speak:

- Members of the class give the teacher commands.
- Students in pairs model and respond for each other.
- Students perform solo for the class, once the teacher is sure they understand the language.

Teaching Welsh through TPR

MORE TO EXPLORE

Books on TPR are available only through Sky Oaks Productions, PO Box 1102, Los Gatos, California 95031, USA tprworld@aol.com

James ASHER **Learning Another Language Through Actions** 1996 (5th edition) *The history of TPR, a huge bibliography, FAQs and a full sample syllabus for 160 hours of English for beginners.*

Ramiro GARCIA **Instructor's Notebook: How to Apply TPR for the Best Results** 1996 (4th edition). *A real teacher's bible full of practical TPR material you can use. Examples are in Spanish, but the book is about method.*

Eric SCHESSLER **English Grammar Through Actions** 1995

www.tpr-world.com

Based on an article by Robin Cain.

SILENT WAY

Caleb Gattegno (1911-1988) taught 'humans-as-energy'. He worked to clarify (a) the inner resources of learning with which human beings are equipped and (b) the right relationship between teaching and learning. In his view teaching should be subordinated to learning, guided by (a) the human potential for learning and (b) each learner's actual learning process as it unfolds. The subject matter is a vehicle for learning rather than the target of the learning. The mastery of the subject matter is a by-product of learning, not a result of teaching. The purpose of the teacher is to create the climate, conditions and opportunities for autonomous learning.

In practice, Gattegno used and developed specific materials to help with the learning process:

- Cuisenaire rods. Coloured rods of different lengths developed by the mathematician Georges Cuisenaire – which are also used for teaching maths.
- A series of charts which identify each separate sound in a language with a different colour. Lists are given of all the different sounds, each in a different colour, giving all possible spellings of each sound. (The English chart includes 'u' for the sound 'f', as in lieutenant!) Words are written out with the letters in the colour for their sound.

The silence comes from the teacher who keeps quiet as much as possible – no long explanations, minimal verbal correction, no excessive praise, minimal modelling of correct sounds. Basically the students are viewed as strong, independent, gifted people, and the teacher does not do things for them that they can work out for themselves.

A sample exchange is the teacher pointing to a sound on the chart and giving one clear model. Students are then encouraged to volunteer. Correct sounds are acknowledged with a smile or a nod, other students are invited to give better models for students who are not yet producing sounds correctly. Individual sounds are tapped out to make words … words are tapped out to make sentences. Sentences are related to actions, mostly using the rods.

Vocabulary is initially limited to words connected with the rods (size, colour), pronouns (*I, you, her, it, them*, etc) and verbs describing what you can do with the rods (*touch, pick up, take*, etc). Students understand grammatical rules deductively and by trial and error as they and the teacher manipulate the rods in clear and unambiguous ways and use appropriate language (simple commands, describing what is happening or has happened, guessing what will happen, etc). The aim is to give students as much help as they need to develop their own criteria as to how the language works and what is acceptable, and to help them become autonomous learners. Later the rods can be used to represent other things: parts of speech, word stress, protagonists and props in stories, etc.

Photo: Manfred Hess

MORE TO EXPLORE

Caleb GATTEGNO **The common sense of teaching foreign languages** Educational Solutions 1976. *The method described by its inventor.*

http://members.aol.com/edusol99/

www.cuisenaire.com *Source of cuisenaire rods.*

MICHEL THOMAS METHOD

Michel Thomas, an exceptional linguist, has developed his oral translation method over a period of 25 years. Only recently has it been published in recorded form.

His published courses consist of recordings of him using English to teach two students the target language – Spanish, French, Italian and German are available. Self-study learners listen and pause the recording to supply their own answers without at any stage making a conscious attempt to learn or remember.

Thomas has broken down each target language into his own easily-understandable classifications and component parts, and by starting with those aspects of the language which are most similar to English and those which follow straightforward patterns, students are able to translate relatively long sentences and complicated ideas within a very short space of time. The method is very intensive, totally learner-focused, and 'mistakes' are accepted as an essential part of the learning process, although Thomas is rigorous in correcting (and explaining) those aspects, especially to do with pronunciation, which will make comprehension difficult.

The method is based on understanding rather than memory, appeals to 'left-brained' learners, is fast-moving, and gives learners (including absolute beginners with no previous language-learning experience) the confidence to speak and a belief in their own ability to learn quickly and easily.

Although this is not traditionally included as a 'humanistic' approach, it is included here because it is completely student-centred.

MORE TO EXPLORE

Nothing published except the recorded courses.

Michel Thomas French, German, Spanish, Italian Hodder & Stoughton 2000

www.michelthomas.com

It might also be of interest to read Michel Thomas's own story of fighting in the French resistance, being captured and tortured by the Gestapo, losing his family in Auschwitz, moving to Los Angeles and eventually becoming language tutor to the rich and famous: **The Test of Courage** *by Christopher Robbins, published by Random House.*

LYDBURY TRIANGLES: A GLOBAL APPROACH

The Lydbury Triangles is not a methodology, it's a holistic way of approaching the content of English grammar. It's included here because it brings up the important question of what we teach, as well as how we teach it. It isn't really enough to go on teaching the same small nuggets of disconnected information in an 'accelerated' way. We need also to look at what information should be presented and how to structure that information in a 'global' way, so that it is comprehensible.

Rita Baker, working at the Lydbury English Centre, has come up with a unique way of giving a complete overview of verb tenses in English on two pages. One shows form, the other meaning.

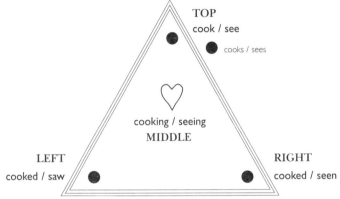

The basis of the form is the triangle. The diagram shows all possible parts of any verb in English, whether regular or irregular. (The only exception, 'to be', has 'am/is/are' at the top, and 'was/were' on the left.)

In compound tenses, the auxiliary verb goes to the left – and shows any changes of person, and the main verb is in an unchanging form on the right. 'To be' (in the active) is always followed by the middle of the triangle (-ing), 'to have' by the right side (past participle), and active three-part tenses always follow the sequence 'have' + 'been' ('to be' as a past participle following 'have') + main verb-ing (following 'be').

There is a simple adjustment to the overall system to show how passives and modals fit the pattern – after which there are no exceptions. The whole thing can be explained in less than an hour. The

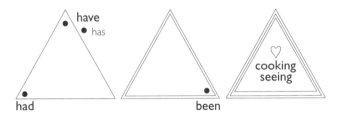

overview of the meanings, to which again there are no exceptions, might take another hour. Playing with them and understanding all the implications does of course take longer, but the value is that all future understanding is in the context of an overall pattern.

It's not that other grammar books are wrong – it's just that the explanations for each individual part of the system do not take account of the whole, and therefore they are partial. Sometimes the wrong part of the explanation is emphasised to fit a particular example. As Rita Baker says, *'Wisdom is knowing what to overlook.'* She is also not claiming to have created a new system, merely to have *'stumbled on a tool that reveals what already exists'*.

MORE TO EXPLORE

Rita BAKER **Lydbury Triangles, A Global Approach to English Verbs and Tenses** Saffire Press 2004. *The book explains it all.*

Thanks to Rita Baker for reading and commenting on this section.   www.lydbury.co.uk

Neuro-Linguistic Programming

Neuro-Linguistic Programming (NLP) is a theory of excellence. It was started in the 1970s by Richard Bandler, John Grinder and others, and has been developing ever since. The starting point was looking for 'the difference that makes the difference' between people who are excellent in their achievements, and those who have not yet achieved excellence. It involves discovering and then **modelling** (copying exactly) everything that 'excellent' people do – the ways they behave and the ways they perceive and interpret the world, which means understanding the different ways in which the brain works. Over time, NLP has been developed and added to by the founders and many others. It consists of **presuppositions** about the way the brain works and the ways in which people react to the world and each other, and numerous tools and techniques for change.

NLP was originally developed as a psychotherapeutic tool, but then it gained a slightly unsavoury reputation when it was picked up by commerce, particularly sales. However it is very effective when used for self-development, and provides significant insights into more effective learning and teaching.

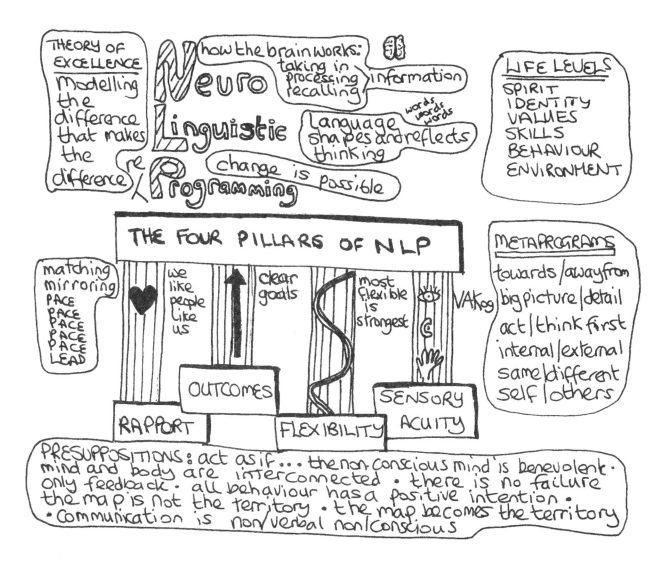

SENSORY PERCEPTION: VAK

Taking in new information We experience the world through our five senses, known in NLP as VAKOG: Visual, Auditory, Kinesthetic (touch and movement), Olfactory and Gustatory. After the age of about 12, most of us have a preference for taking in information through one or two of three of them, V, A or K, although this depends a great deal on what it is we are learning. Although most people can learn through any of the channels, some people have a very strong preference for one and can find it difficult, if not impossible, to take in information unless it is presented in this mode. The people who traditionally fall through the net in our education system are those with a strong kinesthetic preference, and since everyone needs to move in order to learn, it makes sense to incorporate movement whenever new material is presented.

- Know your own preferences. That's probably the way you prefer to teach. Remember to present new information using a range of sensory techniques.
- Incorporate (note the word) movement whenever learners are taking in new information.

Processing and recalling information Our brains also use the five senses to process and recall information. We visualise, talk to ourselves, feel (physically and emotionally), and can bring to mind tastes and smells. Some people have a strong preference for the way they process and recall information, most of us have a preference (which may be different depending on what we're doing), and most of us have a preferred sequence for doing

this. Some of us are more effective than others. You can often notice how people are experiencing the world by the sensory language (predicates) they use: *I've got the weight of the world on my shoulders. (K)* • *Do you see what I mean? (V)* • *That doesn't ring any bells with me. (A)* • *Something smells fishy. (O)* If you want to communicate well with them, **match** the sensory language they are using.

Eye movements can also indicate how a person is thinking. If they are trying to imagine or remember something, they literally look around inside their heads. Where their eyes stop before they focus back on you is where they found it! Looking up usually indicates someone visualising. Looking to the side (or putting one's head on one side) can indicate listening to an internal voice or sounds. Looking down usually indicates someone accessing feelings – or having an internal dialogue. If they're looking to the left (you see the eyes moving to your right) they are usually remembering; to their right they are usually constructing something new (you can therefore sometimes tell if someone may be lying). Not everyone follows this pattern, but most people follow a consistent pattern.

- *The best spellers (in English) are those who visualise. Write new words up high. Encourage learners to look up and visualise words they want to remember.*

It is almost impossible to take in, process and recall information simultaneously. (Try listening to one song while trying to remember another.) That's why it can be easier to think if you close your eyes and shut out external stimuli.

- *Remember to leave time for processing between giving new information and asking people to recall or reproduce it. Processing time varies according to how complicated or foreign the new information is. 'Sleeping on it' helps.*
- *If you want people to be creative, minimise external stimuli.*

Sensory modalities are not learning styles as such (page 33), although they do obviously affect strongly how people learn. Each sensory style – also called a modality – has **submodalities** (page 66).

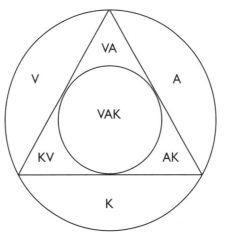

EXPLORE YOUR TEACHING PREFERENCES

Categorise your recent teaching activities. Put one tick in the diagram for each activity reflecting one style, or a combination. What is your preferred style? Can you have more balance in your teaching?

PRESUPPOSITIONS

NLP theory presupposes that the following are true for the way people operate as organisms. (They are not necessarily true for the way society operates.) You do not have to believe them or believe in them, but you will operate more effectively if you act as if they are true. If we act as if the following presuppositions are true, what are the implications for teaching?

- **Mind and body are interconnected.** Thinking can affect the body; the way you hold your body can affect your mind (try slouching and trying to feel happy, then sit up straight and see how much easier it is.)
- **The map is not the territory.** We all have different maps of the world and reality.
- **The map becomes the territory.** What you believe and think about becomes true. It therefore makes sense to focus on the positive, on things you want to happen.

THINK HOW IT WOULD BE IF MIND AND BODY WERE NOT CONNECTED...

From **In Your Hands** by Jane Revell and Susan Norman, pub Saffire Press 1997

Artwork by Mal

- **Communication is both conscious and non-conscious** – in fact, more non-conscious (page 22).
- **Communication is both verbal and non-verbal** – more non-verbal.
- **The non-conscious mind is benevolent.** It is always trying to help us succeed.
- **All behaviour has a positive intention** – for the person carrying out the behaviour. (It may not be positive for others, and there may be better ways of behaving, but everybody is doing their best to succeed as well as they know how.)
- The resources we need are within us. It's just a case of finding and activating them.
- **There is no failure only feedback.** This relates to how the brain learns, it is not about externally imposed tests.
- **The meaning of my communication is the response that I get.** If I want a different response, I must communicate in a different way.

NEURO

how we experience and interpret the world through our five senses, and how the brain works

LINGUISTIC

how the language we use to ourselves and others reflects and shapes our experience of the world

PROGRAMMING

how we can train ourselves (and others) to think, act and speak in new and positive ways; our brains have already been programmed genetically and by our experience; we can re-programme them to act more effectively

The Four Pillars of NLP

Outcomes Being absolutely clear about what you want helps you to get it. One of the most challenging things is often to know precisely what it is we do want. Set clear and precise goals.

Rapport The heart of successful communication with others. To get into rapport you need to pace others, eg by matching or mirroring their body language, their breathing rate, their energy level, etc. We like people like ourselves.

Sensory acuity Using our senses to observe others carefully without assumptions or judgments, so that we can respond appropriately with maximum rapport.

Flexibility Having a range of skills so that you can do something different if what you're doing isn't working. The most successful communicators are those who most successfully deal with change, the ones with the greatest flexibility which comes with knowledge and skill.

Language

There is a very strong link between the language we use and the ways in which we think (which in turn influences how we behave). You can understand a lot about people (including yourself) if you notice the language they are using. As well as the sensory language (page 62), English is full of metaphoric language (page 26).

Labelling people tends to fix our reaction to them. If we call someone a bully, we are defining them in relation to one aspect of their behaviour. How much good cooking do I have to do to be called a good cook? How often does someone have to steal to be labelled a thief? Label and respond to the behaviour, rather than labelling the person.

Reframing can change the way we think about things by changing the words we use. Calling a 'problem' a 'challenge', for example, doesn't change the situation, but at a subtle level can change our attitude to it and therefore our behaviour.

Precision model Being precise with language changes our thinking and behaviour. The **meta-model**, and the simplified version below, the **precision model**, identify ways in which the language we use can block us:

- **Deletions**: *I don't understand. – What exactly don't you understand?*
- **Universal quantifiers** (*always, no-, any-*, etc): *Everybody hates me. – Everybody? Every single person in the world?*
- **Comparative deletions**: *I want to be a better teacher. – Better than what? How much better? In what ways?*
- **Modal operatives of necessity** (*should, must,* etc): *I've got to get this done right now. – What makes it necessary? What would happen if you didn't or couldn't?*
- **Modal operatives of impossibility**: *I can't learn foreign languages. – What stops you? Do you mean 'can't' or 'don't want to' or 'haven't really tried'?*

It is important too when setting goals to be absolutely precise about the outcome you want. Use positive language to describe exactly what you want (rather than what you're trying to avoid), and be precise about the circumstances in which you want it.

METAPROGRAMS

Metaprograms are the in-built programmes which influence our behaviour. (More than 64 clear metaprograms have been identified and there are no doubt countless more.) In these examples, which of the alternatives do you tend to do 'naturally'?

- *Do you act first or think first?*
- *Do you judge your achievement by your own internal standards or according to the praise or blame of others?*
- *Do you want things to be the same, or are you stimulated by the new and different?*
- *Are you driven by your goal, or are you motivated to avoid failure? Do you move towards or away from?*
- *Do you like to be told how to do something or do you like to find your own way?*
- *Do you need to see an overview, before you look at detail, or do you need to follow the step-by-step sequence before you can understand the big picture?*

Whatever your 'natural' preferences, there are other people who do it another way – and they know that 'their way is the right way' (and probably don't know that there might be another way).

> *There's no such thing as a difficult student – just one who doesn't want to do it my way.*

With most of the metaprograms, about 30-40% of people have a strong preference at either end of the spectrum and 20-30% are somewhere in the middle. However, a majority of people need to see the big picture before they can understand the detail, and a high proportion of people are more comfortable with sameness (with some change) to constant change – hence the strong resistance to change in organisations.

If we know what possible modes of behaviour other people think 'normal', we are more likely to be able to understand and react to them with flexibility.

> *If the child is not learning the way you are teaching, then you must teach in the way the child learns.*
> **RITA DUNN**

> *Keep your THOUGHTS positive because your thoughts become your WORDS.*
>
> *Keep your WORDS positive because your words become your ACTIONS.*
>
> *Keep your ACTIONS positive because your actions become your HABITS.*
>
> *Keep your HABITS positive because your habits become your VALUES.*
>
> *Keep your VALUES positive because your values shape your thoughts and create your FUTURE*

NLP now encompasses many different ideas and techniques – many of which overlap (especially in their implications for teaching and learning) with Accelerated Learning. Accessing the non-conscious mind (page 22) is a case in point. The following are some pointers about what else to look out for.

ANCHORING

'Anchors' occur naturally when a particular place, smell, sound, tone of voice, etc, evokes a memory, behaviour pattern or feeling. This natural tendency can be harnessed to break unhelpful anchors (eg fear of all dogs resulting from an incident with one dog) or to create helpful anchors.

Some possible teaching applications are to use consistent colour coding, consistent places for regular occurrences, eg a quiet corner, place where assignments are written up, a 'penalty box' – the one (and only) place in the room from which you administer discipline, etc.

PERCEPTUAL POSITIONS

You get a much clearer view of a situation and possible resolution of conflict by seeing a situation from your own perspective, from the perspective of the 'opposing' point of view, and from the outside as an independent observer.

* *Try evaluating your teaching from all three perceptual positions.*

SUBMODALITIES

When we visualise, we all do different things in our heads. Some see a clear picture, others get a sort of fuzzy feeling, but most people are able to answer questions such as: Does your picture have a border? Is it in black and white or colour? How close to you is it? Are you looking at the picture from the outside (disassociated) or are you in the experience (associated)?   And they are able to manipulate the image: Make it bigger – smaller; closer – further away; stand outside, step inside. All these variations are called submodalities, and there are submodalities for the other senses (modalities) too: Make the sound louder, quieter, higher, lower, etc. Manipulating the submodalities can have a powerful effect on our feelings and subsequent behaviour, and is the basis of many of the therapeutic techniques used in NLP.

> *If you always do what you've always done, you'll always get what you've always got.*

* *Make sure you're associated to good feelings, and disassociated from bad ones. (It can be helpful to disassociate if you have to discipline someone, or talk to them about something about which you have negative feelings.)*
* *Find out how students use their imaginations. It can have a strong impact on their reading abilities.*

TIMELINES

People's concept of time can have a strong influence on their behaviour. Try closing your eyes and bringing to mind a memorable event yesterday, something last week, something last year. Physically point to each event. Then do the same for three future events. Can you now plot your timeline? If you find you are not actually on your timeline, you may feel that 'life is passing you by'. Try physcally moving so that you are on it and see how that affects how you view the world. People who 'can't see the future' may find that their future is behind them. The simple thing is to turn round. (Sounds crazy, but it seems to work.)

LIFE LEVELS

Also called Logical Levels. We operate more efficiently and happily if all aspects of our lives are in harmony. The levels are: **environment, behaviour, abilities, beliefs, identity (sense of self), spirit.**

MORE TO EXPLORE

Richard BANDLER & John GRINDER **Frogs into princes** Real People Press 1979. *Where it all started. A summary of therapy sessions.*

Richard BANDLER **Using your brain for a change** Real People Press 1985. *By one of the founders of NLP.*

Jane REVELL & Susan NORMAN **In Your Hands** Saffire Press 1997. *Introduction, with exercises, stories and guided visualisations, slanted towards teaching and learning.*

Jane REVELL & Susan NORMAN **Handing Over** Saffire Press 1999. *Suggestions, lesson plans and teaching techniques based on NLP, mainly geared towards teaching foreign languages.*

So what does it mean?

NLP contains lots of different meanings, but its main message is that people are different. Some are more effective at doing certain things than others. By learning the skills others use, we can improve our own performance.

NLP identifies our 'default position' – what we tend to do naturally. Start by finding out how your own brain works, understand how other people's brains might work differently, and then adapt your teaching to take account of all the different ways people take in information, process information and behave.

Remember though, when you looked through all the questions about how your brain works, your most frequent answer was probably 'it depends'. It depends on what I'm doing, how I'm feeling, how familiar I am with the subject, and on a host of other things. Most people are not polarized at one end of the spectrum or the other, they are somewhere in the middle. Although we have preferences and ways of working which are more comfortable for us, we can work in many different ways. The difficulties come when teachers get stuck into one way, especially when it is fairly near one end of the spectrum and they are trying to teach students who are near the other end.

We are not talking about classifying learners as 'visuals', 'kinesthetics', 'big picture people' etc, especially if it results in dividing them into groups and teaching them only in that way. We are only talking about producing specific learning profiles and programmes for individual children when they have such strong learning preferences that they can only learn in one way. These are often the children who are already being catered for because they have been picked up as having 'learning difficulties' – although the difficulties often disappear when they are taught in more appropriate ways. Most people can learn under the most difficult of conditions – but they learn much more quickly and easily if conditions are more favourable. The key to teaching a group of different individuals is to …

…**Offer Choice** Let people work on different activities or the same activity at different levels. *'Here's the task, you can either do it this way or in your own way. You've got 30 minutes to achieve this result.' 'Here are 12 questions. Everyone do the first two, plus eight others.'* (You go through them all afterwards.) *'Here are the six essays to write and the dates they must be in by. You choose the order in which you write them.'*

Joseph O'Connor & Ian McDermott **Principles of NLP** Thorsons-HarperCollins 1996. *General introduction.*

Joseph O'Connor & John Seymour **Introducing NLP** Thorsons-HarperCollins 1993. *General introduction.*

Diana BEAVER **NLP for Lazy Learning** (previously 'Lazy learning') Vega-Chrysalis Books Group 2002 and **Easy Being** Useful Book Company 1997. *Focus on teaching and learning.*

Sue KNIGHT **NLP at work** (1995) and **NLP Solutions** (1999) Nicholas Brealey. *Business applications of NLP.*

Shelley Rose CHARVET **Words that change minds** Kendall/Hunt. *The language to use to influence people with many different metaprograms.*

Michael GRINDER **Righting the Educational Conveyor Belt** Metamorphous Press 1991. *NLP excellence in the classroom.*

www.anlp.org *Association for Neuro-Linguistic Programming*

nlpednet@new-oceans.co.uk *NLP in Education Network*

inlpta@btclick.com *International Neuro-Linguistic Programming Trainer's Association*

Nonviolent Communication

The giraffe has the largest heart of any living land mammal, which is why Marshall Rosenberg took it as the symbol of compassionate communication in which people express their feelings, needs and requests while respecting the feelings, needs and requests of others. He called this the language of Nonviolent Communication (NVC). The language of criticism and judgment, is symbolised by the jackal.

THE PROCESS

- **Observation** Describe what you see or hear. Be specific, without evaluating the action and without judging the person.
- **Feeling** Express how you feel in response to the observed event. Typical feelings are angry, afraid, confused, sad, worried, embarrassed, lonely, numb, tired, surprised, uncomfortable. NVC avoids 'feeling' words which carry an implied judgment or criticism of the other person, eg betrayed, patronised, used, rejected, cheated, diminished. Nobody makes you feel anything. What they do or say may stimulate a feeling in you, but not cause it. Feelings are related to needs. If we feel anxious or afraid, it is because one of our basic needs is not being met. (Marshall's book provides extensive lists of genuine and judgmental feeling words.)
- **Need** Needs are the 'root of our feelings'. Some basic human needs are the need for autonomy (freedom to choose for oneself), for celebration, for integrity, for interdependence (eg for acceptance, appreciation, community, love, respect), for physical nurturing (food, protection, shelter, physical contact, sex), for play, and for spiritual communion (beauty, harmony, inspiration, order and peace).
- **Request** Request the other person to do something. Make sure it is a genuine request (which they are then free to turn down), rather than a demand. Sometimes demands are disguised as request, but are usually revealed by the reaction (anger, punishment, etc) if they are turned down.

The language we use as teachers and trainers has a great effect on learners, as does the language they use to one another. NVC is a really useful approach for helping us clean up the language we use with learners, colleagues, friends and family.

FEELING WORDS when needs are *not* met

afraid • annoyed • angry • appalled • confused • disconnected • dislike • disquiet • embarrassed • grief • hurt • lonely • miserable • numb • regretful • resentful • sad • shaky • tense • tired • vulnerable • worried

---

FEELING WORDS when needs *are* met

affectionate • alert • calm • confident • curious • energetic • enthusiastic • grateful • happy • hopeful • inspired • joyful • peaceful • pleased • rejuvenated • relieved • secure • sympathetic • trusting • vibrant • warm

---

MORE TO EXPLORE

Marshall ROSENBERG **Nonviolent Communication – a language of compassion** Puddle Dancer Press 1999

www.cnvc.org

Spiral Dynamics

Spiral Dynamics (SD) is a model developed by Clare W Graves (1914-1986) which offers insights into how people think and behave. His model is of adult (13 years plus) human psychological development which applies both to individuals and to groups and cultures. The model is continually being developed by others.

The spiral starts at the bottom with the colour **beige** and moves up to the eighth level, **turquoise**. The next level, **coral**, has not yet been accepted by everyone, although it has been suggested that there are actually 24 levels in total.

Typically through their lives as they grow and develop, people move up through the levels, which become increasingly complex, with each incorporating all aspects of earlier levels. But in new or stressful situations, they may drop (hopefully temporarily) to a lower level. Alternate sides of the spiral are characterised as warm 'expressive' systems which are self referenced (**beige**, **red**, **orange**, **yellow**), or cool 'sacrificial' systems which are externally referenced and serve others. Change from one level to the next occurs when one is no longer comfortable in the current level and change may therefore be preceded by a period of unease and discomfort. There is a qualitative difference in worldview when making the move from the **green** to the **yellow** level.

When teaching others, it is necessary for the teacher to be at a sufficiently advanced stage to be able to relate appropriately to those 'below' – and to be aware of what people at each level require of them.

MORE TO EXPLORE

C Cowan & D Beck **Spiral Dynamics: Mastering leadership, Values & Change** Blackwell 1996

www.spiraldynamics.net

www.spiraldynamics.org

www.spiraldynamicsgroup.com

CORAL … this level is posited as the next stage of development

TURQUOISE (Sacrifice to save the planet) Holistic view. Desire for spiritual dimension, living in harmony and balance. Accepting existential dichotomies.

YELLOW (Self – knowledge) Integrative, systematic. Seeking to understand the complexities of the systems within which one lives.

GREEN (Sacrifice to reach consensus) Co-operation, egalitarian. Need to build a better world for all.

ORANGE (Self – manipulation) Strategy. Express self, but in a manner acceptable to others. Negotiation. Win-win.

BLUE (Sacrifice for truth) Purposeful, authoritarian. Deferred gratification. There is one right way. Seeking order, meaning and purpose.

RED (Self – power) Egocentric, impulsive. Taking the role of warrior aggressor in a hostile world.

PURPLE (Sacrifice for the tribe) Need for repetition and rituals as protection from unknowable world. Importance of the group/tribe.

BEIGE (Self) Basic survival level. Instinctive. Adults rarely come into this category unless seriously ill or in extreme emotional distress.

Seven Levels of Consciousness

In 1997, Richard Barrett developed a series of assessment tools which can be used by individuals or groups such as families, schools, business organisations and nations. The tools map values to the 'seven levels of consciousness' model, which was developed from Abraham Maslow's Hierarchy of Needs (page 16), substituting 'states of consciousness' for 'hierarchy of needs' and expanding the concept of self-actualisation. Balance at all levels of the model is an indication of health, well-being and sustainability.

The beliefs associated with each of the seven existential needs are the principal motivating forces in all human affairs. Individuals grow in consciousness by learning how to integrate the beliefs that allow them successfully to master each life need. Individuals who master all the life needs operate from full-spectrum consciousness. They have the ability to respond appropriately to all life's challenges.

The beliefs associated with the 'lower' needs (1-3) deal with the practical aspects of living in the external world. Individuals and groups who focus only on the development of the lower life needs are unable to find fulfilment because they do not know how to bring meaning to their lives. The beliefs associated with the upper life needs (4-7) deal with the spiritual aspects of life – the internal world. Individuals and groups who focus only on the upper life themes are unable to reach their full potential because they lack the skills to operate effectively in the physical world.

The seven levels of consciousness

Theme	Stage	PERSONAL Motivation	SCHOOL Motivation	CORPORATE Motivation
Service	7	Serving humanity and the planet	Societal awareness and involvement	Global vision and service to humanity
Inclusion	6	Making a difference in people's lives	Local community awareness and involvement	Partnerships with customers, suppliers and local community
Cohesion	5	Bringing meaning to existence	Shared vision and values, commitment and enthusiasm	Shared vision and values in the company
Transformation	4	Aligning self-interest with collective interest	Continuous renewal. Faculty, parent and student participation in school governance	Self-knowledge and continuous renewal
Self-esteem	3	Being respected by one's peers	Systems and rules that promote school order and effectiveness	Best practice and a desire for greatness
Relationships	2	Developing loving relationships	Harmonious student, faculty and parent relationships	Harmonious interpersonal relationships and good communications
Survival	1	Ensuring physical safety	Financial soundness and personal security	Financial survival, profit

WHAT IS CONSCIOUSNESS?

Barrett describes consciousness as 'awareness with purpose'. Consciousness must have a vehicle; it cannot exist on its own. Consciousness becomes apparent when entities display behaviours with a purpose. All purposes are a function of self-interest. So-called altruistic purposes are driven by an entity's need to find meanings, make a difference or be of service. Values are the concepts that provide a shorthand method of describing beliefs and behaviours.

Thanks to Richard Barrett for his comments.

MORE TO EXPLORE

Richard BARRETT A Guide to Liberating Your Soul Fulfilling Books 1995; Liberating the Corporate Soul: Building a Visionary Organization Butterworth Heinemann 1998; Love, Fear and the Destiny of Nations: Evaluating the Impact of the Evolution of Human Consciousness on Business and World Affairs forthcoming 2004

www.valuescentre.com

www.corptools.com

Go to the valuescentre website to take part in an international values assessment survey.

Transactional Analysis

Developed by Eric Berne (1910-1970), TA asserts that all of us typically act and communicate from three positions: Parent, Adult, Child. The parent/child states are learnt in childhood and each has positive and negative attributes (Nurturing Parent, Controlling Parent; Free Child, Adapted Child). Although we might move in and out of all five states from time to time, the most healthy state for all parties involved in communication is the adult state – behaviours, thoughts and feelings which are direct responses to the here and now. Problems arise when adults – typically couples – get 'stuck' into habitual ways of behaving. 'Adaptive child' and 'controlling parent' are rarely appropriate states for healthy adult communication.

> **Philosophical assumptions**
> * People are OK.
> * Everyone has the capacity to think.
> * People decide their own destiny, and decisions can be changed.

OTHER TA CONCEPTS

Scripts Our personalities are virtually fully formed by the time we are seven, and after this time we subconsciously live out 'scripts', ie life plans which are strongly influenced by messages we receive prior to the age of seven.

Discounting Non-conscious selective ignoring of information so our script coincides with our perception of reality.

Racketeering Showing feelings with which we feel comfortable to mask what we really feel.

Strokes Any act of recognition during a communicative transaction is a 'stroke'. Typically we all react better to positive strokes, but if they are not available, then any stroke is better than being ignored (children sometimes behave badly so that adults will at least take notice of them).

Autonomy The awareness, spontaneity and capacity for intimacy which is the 'adult' goal of TA.

Drivers There are five main motivators, known as 'drivers', which are learnt in childhood. All of them are useful in moderation, but can cause problems when they become to strong. Which one (or two, or more) of these do you recognise in relation to yourself and others?

Please me • Try hard • Be strong • Hurry up • Be perfect

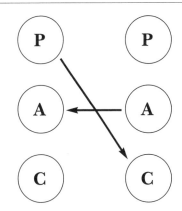

THE EGO-STATE MODEL

Adult (behaving, thinking, feeling in response to what is going on around me in the here and now)

Parent (behaving, thinking, feeling in ways that are a copy of my parent/s or parent figures)

Child (ways of behaving, thinking, feeling that I used when I was a child)

MORE TO EXPLORE

Vann JOINES & Ian STEWART TA Today Lifespan 1987

Eric BERNE Transactional Analysis in Psychotherapy Grove Press 1961

Eric BERNE Games People Play Penguin 1964

www.ita.org.uk Institute of Transactional Analysis

www.itaa-net.org

www.ta-tutor.com

The Enneagram

The Enneagram (pronounced any-agram) is a nine-point model of personality types which shows how we function at different levels of development – and how we shift styles at times of growth and times of stress.

We each correspond to one of the numbers, and our personality may be generally more towards the positive or negative characteristics of each, but also may show all those characteristics in different conditions. As we develop, we tend to move forward to the next number in the sequence. Note that there are two separate sequences which do not interact:

1 – 7 – 5 – 8 – 2 – 4 – 1

or **9 – 3 – 6 – 9**

If you are at 7, for example, you will develop to 5, while still retaining aspects of your original number. Under pressure, you will exhibit the negative traits of your primary number, or may regress to the previous number in the sequence.

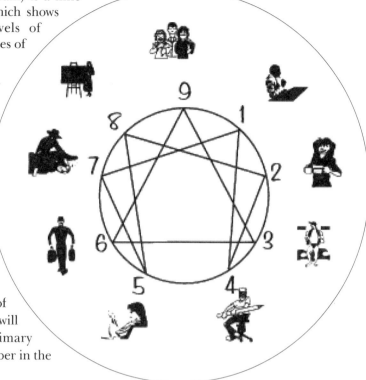

THE NINE TYPES

Type 1 The Reformer / The Perfectionist

Rational, idealistic, perfectionist, self-righteous *Margaret Thatcher*

Type 2 The Helper / The Giver

Nurturing, concerned, possessive, manipulative *Mother Teresa*

Type 3 The Motivator / The Performer

Self-assured, adaptive, image-conscious, deceiver *Tony Robbins*

Type 4 The Individualist / The Tragic Romantic

Intuitive, expressive, self-absorbed, depressive *Judy Garland*

Type 5 The Investigator / The Observer

Perceptive, conceptualiser, detached, reclusive *Bill Gates*

Type 6 The Loyalist / The Devil's Advocate

Endearing, responsible, evasive, paranoid *Princess Diana*

Type 7 The Enthusiast / The Epicure

Enthusiastic, fun loving, excessive, manic *Robin Williams*

Type 8 The Leader / The Boss

Assertive, decisive, aggressive, ruthless *Saddam Hussein*

Type 9 The Peacemaker / The Mediator

Receptive, supportive, self-effacing, dissociated *Ronald Reagan*

In the boxed summary of each type, the first name for each type is the one used by Don Richard Riso and Russ Hudson and the second is Helen Palmer's. The words which follow are descriptions of the type, going from healthy to unhealthy. Finally there is an example of a famous person who Riso suggests may be representative of the type (you decide whether healthy or unhealthy).

Based on an article by Julie Hay.

MORE TO EXPLORE

Don Richard RISO with Russ Hudson **Personality Types** Houghton Mifflin (revised edition) 1996

Helen PALMER **The Enneagram** Harper 1991

Myers Briggs Type Indicator®

The Myers Briggs personality questionnaire is a psychometric test which gives insights into the meaning behind our actions, what motivates us, why we react in the ways we do, the deeper esoteric meanings of our lives and how we can learn to understand and live and work with others. It was developed originally by Katherine Briggs, from the work of Carl Jung, and then developed further by her daughter, Isabel Briggs Myers.

The Myers Briggs Type Indicator measures eight different types of behavioural characteristics arranged on four bi-polar scales. At the end of each scale is one of two behaviours which are the bi-polar opposite of the other, and where the middle represents a balance between the two.

This first extraversion/introversion scale illustrates where we like to focus our attention and energy. Scores towards introversion indicate a tendency to be pulled inwards to reflect on our own ideas and concepts; extraversion indicates that our attention may be more often pulled outwards, meaning that other people and things are more attractive than our own inner thoughts.

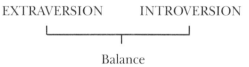

The second scale represents the way we take in information, which means it can have considerable implications in understanding the way we like to learn. Sensing people like to start at the beginning, learning step by step and building up information gradually, detail by detail. Intuitives prefer to build up information by looking at the big picture, jumping in anywhere, leaping over several steps at a time, and processing information instantaneously.

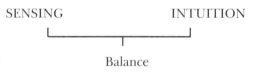

The third scale represents the way we like to make decisions. Thinkers like to make decisions through applying logic and analysis, and being task orientated and firm minded. Feelers like to make decisions through person-centred values such as being supportive, compassionate, harmonious and taking personal convictions into consideration.

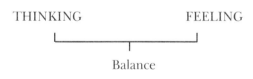

The fourth and last scale is indicative of the way we like to organise our lives. Judging types like to be planned and methodical, and have a definite order and structure to their lives. Perceivers like to be more flexible, spontaneous, adaptable and to go with the flow.

MORE TO EXPLORE

www.personalitypage.com *Access to Myers Briggs and other personality type indicators.*

Based on an article by Shirley Laflin.

Belbin Team Role Analysis

One of the best known systems for identifying the types of personality in terms of their ability to work in teams is the team role analysis tool developed by Meredith Belbin. Different teams might need a different combination of types at different times, but any large organisation needs all of them. It is also useful for identifying how and why different learners work together with varying degrees of success. Belbin defines a team role as '*a tendency to behave, contribute and interrelate with others in a particular way*'.

	CONTRIBUTIONS	ALLOWABLE WEAKNESS
PLANT PL	Creative, imaginative, unorthodox. Solves difficult problems.	Ignores incidentals. Too pre-occupied to communicate effectively.
CO-ORDINATOR CO	Mature, confident, good chair. Clarifies goals, promotes decision-making, delegates well.	May be seen as manipulative. Off-loads personal work.
MONITOR EVALUATOR ME	Sober, strategic and discerning. Sees all options. Judges accurately.	Lacks drive and ability to inspire others.
IMPLEMENTER IMP	Disciplined, reliable, conservative and efficient. Turns ideas into practical actions.	Somewhat inflexible. Slow to respond to new possibilities.
COMPLETER FINISHER CF	Painstaking, conscientious, anxious. Searches out errors and omissions. Delivers on time.	Inclined to worry unduly. Reluctant to delegate.
RESOURCE INVESTIGATOR RI	Extrovert, enthusiastic, communicative. Explores opportunities. Develops contacts.	Over-optimistic. Loses interest once initial enthusiasm has passed.
SHAPER SH	Challenging, dynamic, thrives on pressure. Has drive and courage to overcome obstacles.	Prone to provocation. Offends people's feelings.
TEAMWORKER TW	Co-operative, mild, perceptive and diplomatic. Listens, builds, averts friction.	Indecisive in crunch situations.
SPECIALIST SP	Single-minded, self-starting, dedicated. Provides knowledge and skills in rare supply..	Contributes only on a narrow front. Dwells on technicalities.

MORE TO EXPLORE
www.belbin.com

Theory of Constraints (TOC)

The Theory of Constraints is a philosophy of thinking and problem solving that first came to prominence in the 1980s. It was developed by Eliyahu Goldratt, an Israeli physicist and philosopher turned business guru. Drawing heavily on the Socratic Method, both the philosophy and the thinking tools it enshrines were introduced to the world at large in a 'parable-novel' by Goldratt entitled *The Goal*. The book became and remains a best seller.

TOC for Education was founded in 1995 as a non-profit international foundation dedicated to working to improve education for children of all ages.

Constraints are anything which impede learning, and the 'tools' are designed to overcome these barriers. Tools include:

• **The Target Tree** which analyses the steps needed to accomplish goals
• **The Branch** for analysing consequences
• **The Cloud** for conflict resolution

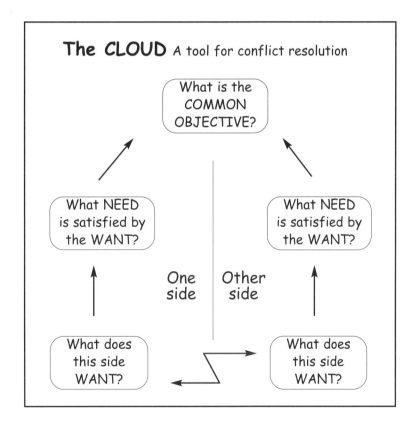

MORE TO EXPLORE

Eliyahu M Goldratt **The Goal** The North River Press 1984. *Global principles of manufacturing in the form of a novel.*

www.tocforeducation.com *Thinking skills tools for children.*

Solutions Focus

Solutions Focus is a change-and-development methodology with a difference. Instead of focusing on what's wrong and figuring out what to do about it, the emphasis instead is on focusing on when the 'right' things happen, and how. This can have a transforming effect on all kinds of situations from corporate change to classroom management to working with schizophrenics. It is used in education, business, social welfare, addiction treatment, prison, group therapy and many other settings around the world.

The method derives from Solution Focused Brief Therapy, devised by Steve de Shazer, Insoo Kim Berg and others in the 1980s and 1990s. This is itself derived from Ericksonian psychotherapy, with a combination of careful use of language and sharp observation. The approach values simplicity in philosophy and language and aims to discover 'what works' in a given situation, simply and practically. The focus on solutions (not problems), the future (not the past) and on what's going well (rather than what's gone wrong) leads to a positive and pragmatic way to work with organisations and individuals.

> *Solutions come easily to a mind uncluttered by complications and limitations.*

Sometimes the very simplicity of the approach can appear daunting and almost naïve. Nonetheless with skilful use, research has shown it to be effective in therapeutic and other applications. In the 15 studies published to date, clients reported improvement in 60-80% of cases. These studies have been carried out in a wide variety of settings, including school behaviour problems, anger management, occupational health and rehabilitation, and problem drinking. These figures are as good as or better than comparative treatments, and were mostly achieved in between just one and five sessions.

On a scale of one to ten, where are you now in relation to your chosen situation?

What positive skills and behaviour allow you to be at this level and not less?

How can you do more of that?

Ask the miracle question:

Suppose the problem vanished overnight. Suppose the situation was suddenly ideal. How would you know that the transformation had happened? What would things be like?

MORE TO EXPLORE

Insoo Kim BERG & Peter de JONG **Interviewing for Solutions** Wadsworth 2001 (2nd ed). *An introduction from one of the originators.*

Paul Z JACKSON and Mark McKERGOW **The Solutions Focus: The SIMPLE Way to Positive Change** Nicholas Brealey Publishing 2002. *Clear overall introduction – aimed at corporate and organisational change.*

John RHODES and Yasmin AJMAL **Solution Focused Thinking in Schools** BT Press 2001. *Introduction to SF in educational settings.*

Linda METCALF **Teaching Toward Solutions** Crown House Publishing 2003. *What it means practically to use Sf in schools.*

Michelle WEINER-DAVIS **Change Your Life and Everyone In It** Simon & Schuster 1996. *Self-help with a solutions focus.*

www.brieftherapy.org.uk *The Brief Therapy Practice, London – SF training for education and therapy.*

www.solworld.org *SOL conferences for SF practitioners in business and organisations.*

www.brieftherapysydney.com.au *Michael Durrant's excellent weblinks to SF resources.*

Contributed by Mark McKergow.

PhotoReading

How long does it 'normally' take you to read a book? Three to six hours spread out over a number of days? And how much of that can you remember? About 10% to tell someone else about, but with an awareness of what else is in the book so you could find it if necessary?

PhotoReading is not about developing a photographic memory. It is not a magic system whereby someone quotes a page number and line to you and you can tell them what it says. It *is* a magic system whereby you can achieve in less than 30 minutes the same results you would normally get after your three to six hours. (Times obviously depend on how big the book is and how new the subject is to you.)

THE BASIC STEPS

1 **GOAL** Decide what you want to get out of the book. Why are you reading it?

2 **OVERVIEW** Spend about three minutes looking at the book – the title, introduction, cover blurb, and just flicking through to get a feeling for the book.

3 **ATTENTION** Focus your attention on a point about 20cm above and slightly behind your head (the tip of a wizard's hat). Relax.

4 **DE-FOCUS** Put the book flat on the table in front of you. Open it. Look at the central spine making sure that the whole book is within your peripheral vision, and let your eyes go slightly out of focus (like looking at a 3D picture).

5 **FORWARDS** Turn the pages one at a time at the rate of about one per second, keeping your eyes de-focused on the centre.

6 **BACKWARDS** When you get to the last page, turn the book upside down and go through it backwards and upside down. (Apparently the brain doesn't mind.)

7 **IGNORE** Forget about the whole thing and do something else for at least 30 minutes. (Preferably sleep on it.)

8 **ACTIVATE** Activate what your brain has taken in by mindmapping or jotting down notes. Or waiting till you need the information and finding how much you didn't realise you knew!

9 **SPEED READ** If you want to make the information more immediately available, then you can speed read as a follow-up activity: go through the book skimming down each page following your finger as it moves quickly down the middle of the page.

The reason it works is that the non-conscious mind takes in information very quickly – although it only comes to conscious awareness when you need it (page 22), hence the need for knowing your goal before you start. Only 4% of vision is light being received by the eye – the rest is manufactured in the brain through our other senses and through kinesthetic/emotional reactions. Also books are usually over-written – things are said more than once in different ways; and you probably know a lot of the information, so you're only looking for the things you don't know.

The more you do it, the more you learn to trust the process – and the benefits are enormous! If there were only one SEAL approach that I wish I'd known when I was at university, it would be PhotoReading!

MORE TO EXPLORE

Paul SCHEELE **PhotoReading** Learning Strategies Corporation 1999. *The book!*

Rhizomatic Learning

Arborescent (tree-type) modes of thinking start from a central trunk and branch outwards. They grow, but they are inherently static, rooted in one central thesis. Rhizomatic connections are networks where connections can be made between any of the individual parts. Rhizomatic plants (often classed as pernicious weeds!) are those that spread through the root system; if any part is destroyed, all other parts can still survive. Rhizomatic thinking is more fluid, creative and innovative.

Rhizomatic learning, which links with a cross-curricular approach, is how everything is interrelated. Although this book is written under separate headings, all the subjects are very much interrelated. Check for yourself.

How does each of these topics relate to all the others?

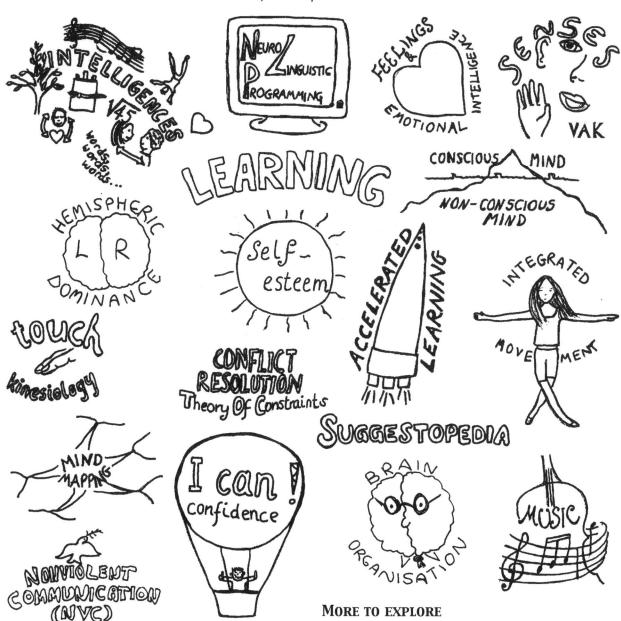

MORE TO EXPLORE

http://athena.english.vt.edu *Go to their creative writing section. Very thought-provoking. Lots of teaching ideas.*

Thanks to Jan Cisek for this information; Artwork Justina Langley.

Quantum Science

What has quantum science to do with learning? Everything. Our whole society is based on the 'proof' provided by scientists of how things are, but it takes time for scientists to provide proof that is generally accepted, and even longer for the new understandings to translate into action. Quantum science has been around for about 100 years, and yet it is still far from being the basis of our society and most people don't know anything about it. It is a huge subject, which impacts on such questions as the interrelatedness of all things, psychic phenomena, the nature of spirituality, the power of collective and individual thought and intention, and the very nature of consciousness (the subject of SEAL's 2003 conference), all of which has immense implications for learning. Just consider the one suggestion that learning is organic (arising from the needs of the individual) rather than imposed from outside. Consider the summary of implications below and consider how this might affect your own life, your learning and your teaching.

OLD PARADIGM	NEW PARADIGM	IMPLICATIONS
Determinism	Indeterminism	
Machine	Organism	*Each present moment is open to new opportunity*
Separate units	Interconnection	*Relation to the world is modelled on relation to living creatures*
Atoms	Fields	*Empathy, for people and other-than-humans, is physically real*
Exact quantities	Articulated structure	*Each of my actions propagates infinite effects*
Observation	Interaction	*My sensitivity to patterns is key to understanding*
Control	Participation	*I accept being changed by what I encounter*
Competition	Co-operation	*I am committed to engagement with the world*
Freedom is illusory	Creativity	*I look for mutual benefit*
		I am willing to shift to new ways of perceiving

Chris Clarke from Proceedings of 9th International SEAL Conference 2001 *Opening Minds to Holistic Learning*

> *All truth goes through three stages.*
> *First it is ridiculed.*
> *Then it is violently opposed.*
> *Finally it is accepted as self-evident.*
>
> SCHOPENHAUER

MORE TO EXPLORE

Lynne McTAGGART **The Field – the quest for the secret force of the universe** Harper Collins 2001. *A collation of scientific evidence proving the importance of the Zero Point Field, an ocean of microscopic vibrations which appear to connect everything in the universe.*

Peter RUSSELL **From Science to God – the mystery of consciousness and the meaning of light** New World Library 2000. *Blending physics, psychology and philosophy, a new worldview in which consciousness is fundamental to the cosmos, where science and spirit no longer conflict.*

Michael TALBOT **The Holographic Universe** HarperCollins 1991. *A vision of the universe as a hologram – and the implications.*

Jeremy NARBY **Cosmic Serpent – DNA and the origins of knowledge** Phoenix 1999. *Links between the knowledge of the ancients and modern science.*

Hal Zina BENNETT, Stanislav GROF **The Holotropic mind: the three levels of human consciousness and how they shape our lives** Harper SanFrancisco 1993. *Exploration of consciousness.*

Afterword

This book is an attempt to give an introduction to the many areas which might be of interest to those involved in the exploration of how human beings operate, how we learn, and therefore how we should be teaching and training, and even how we should be organising our educational and teaching establishments. It is by no means comprehensive, but it is a starting point. It is not a coherent proposal for how we should teach. SEAL does not promote a method. SEAL members do not claim to have all the answers. We hope we are asking some of the right questions.

The 'More to Explore' sections are an integral part of the message. They are the gateway to the next steps in the adventure. Each book and website contains references to direct you further. Enjoy the quest!

There are many different theories and ways of classifying human beings and human behaviour. Ultimately though people do not fit neatly into categories. We all work differently from one another, and we all behave differently in different situations, on different days, with different people – and hopefully we're all learning and therefore changing from day to day, if not from minute to minute. So while the classifications are useful as a way of opening our minds to other possibilities, they lose their usefulness as soon as we start using them to classify people. Models are just models.

The important things are to keep an open mind and to keep learning. The place to start is with yourself – and a sense of humour will be useful!

We have a simple-minded view of other people. It is inevitable – and tragic – that we try to type others with a single number for intelligence or a single adjective, like 'nice' or 'aggressive', as if people could be reduced to one characteristic.

The problem for scientists is to understand this diverse and complex human mental system without trying to quickly come up with another neat model for it. We were built without a neat and well-organised plan (and probably would have been rejected by computer simulation scientists), built with different priorities over many eras. Each one of us is a crowd of people.

Robert Ornstein in **Multimind**

... academiomemesis – the disorder that makes one think a human being is really like a small academic. In this condition a living human being is usually thought to consist of the pure verbal and logical processes. A victim of this disorder gives little attention to the many other dimensions of the person – feelings, personal concerns, bodily needs, the ability to sing and dance, or the ability to get along with many different kinds of people. But funny as it may seem, this limited view is no joke. It is the dominant view of what is known as 'the western intellectual tradition', a view that might be remembered by its acronym, TWIT.

Robert Ornstein in **Multimind**

MORE TO EXPLORE

Robert ORNSTEIN Multimind – a new way of looking at human behaviour Macmillan 1986

Index

The Rickter Company

1 2 3 4 5 6 7 8 9 (10)

Introducing the Rickter Scale®: offering individuals the means to explore possibility, make informed choices, take ownership of their goals and contribute to their own action plan.

Rick Hutchinson and Keith Stead have developed a powerful guidance framework, enabling you to work more effectively with individuals, and to measure their 'soft outcomes' & distance travelled.

By combining a solutions-focused model with the unique Rickter Scale® we can provide you with a tailor made assessment and action planning package.

Cutting edge!!

Our guidance model combines the best practice in motivational interviewing, neuro-lingustic programming, emotional intelligence training and systems thinking.

The Rickter Scale®

The Rickter Scale® is a groundbreaking multi - sensory assessment tool, ideal for use in one to one counselling/coaching, social inclusion, mentoring/supervision/appraisal, team working ….and much more. The Rickter Scale® engages and motivates while remaining non-judgemental.

Taking responsibility

Using the Rickter Scale®, individuals can set realistic and achievable goals, create an action plan and determine the appropriate level of support they require.

Value-added

Data from Rickter Scale® interviews can be used to evidence value for money and demonstrate to both management and funders 'what works'.

Frames of Reference

The Rickter Company will work with you to provide Frames of Reference that reflect the specific needs of your client group and your own way of working. A library of sample Frames of Reference is available via our website www.rickterscale.com.

For more information please contact

The Rickter Company
10 View Place
Inverness
IV2 4SA

Tel: **+44 (0) 1463 717177**
Fax: **+44 (0) 1463 718965**

Email: *info@rickterscale.com*
Web: *www.rickterscale.com*

Mind the Gap . . .

At Stretch Learning, we bridge the gap between the deliverer and the receiver in any given communication situation – and some more.

We stretch people by engaging them totally in the learning process and enabling them to apply what they are learning to their personal and professional lives and to achieve results.

Thanks to us, learning becomes an enjoyable and unforgettable experience.

SOME OF OUR SERVICES
- Learning & development consultancy
- Keynote speaking
- Learning event planning
- Research & design
- Handovers

SOME OF OUR CLIENTS
BT
The Body Shop
Business Objects
Cabinet Office
Four Square
NMEC
Scoot(UK)
Oxford Brookes University
University of Northumbria
Diageo

+44 (0)1494 443 554
Learnmore@stretchlearning.com

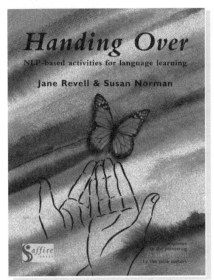

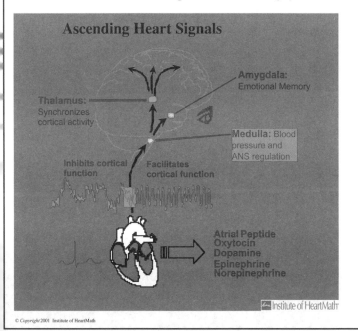

Unfolding in the Scottish Highlands

Anisa Caine set up *Peak Potential* in response to her experience in education, training and consultancy in three continents. In the Highlands of Scotland, surrounded by unspoiled nature and tranquility, she facilitates the development of individuals in their quest for higher levels of excellence. Her clients include artists, writers, educators, CEOs, and HR managers.

She believes that
- Human potential is infinite
- Intellect and emotion must be harmonized by Spiritual Intelligence
- Struggle is a sign of imbalance.

Her special interests include Relationships, Thinking, Communication, Creativity and Meditation. An artist and facilitator, her lifelong interest in Spiritual Intelligence makes her the ideal guide in a 1-to-1 session.

For more details of how you can come to define your goals and acquire the tools you need to achieve them, contact:

PE⅄K
POTENTIAL
Neadaich
Glen Road
Newtonmore
PH20 1DZ
Scotland
TEL +44 1540 673 288
FAX +44 1540 673 998
anisa@dircon.co.uk

Personal Development for Professional Development

Workshops for education, training or communication:

Suggestopedia with Lonny Gold

an exciting redefinition of teaching and learning

Acquire the vision, inner resources and subtle techniques to spark excitement in learning and ensure extraordinary results. Create in your learners those "instants of recognition" that are defining moments in any person's life.

- Get to the essence of teaching and communicating
- Discover how to present information in a brain-friendly way
- Create environments that are both magical and safe
- Design activities that awaken the reserve capacities of the brain

Become the instructor your learners have always dreamed of!

Lonny's workshops are a succession of quick-moving, thought-provoking and entertaining activities that will remain with you for a long time afterwards.

Lonny Gold is probably one of the most experienced Suggestopedic trainers. A Suggestopedic language teacher since 1978 and teacher trainer since 1984, he was the founding president of France's Conseil national de Suggestologie. He authors his own material, and works in all corners of the world. Lonny's deepest belief is "When a teacher looks after the learners, the learning looks after itself."

Detailed proposals: *e-mail* - lonny@going-for-gold.net • *web-site* – www.going-for-gold.net

Bringing Accelerated Learning to Life

Why not join Kimberley Hare and guests on our next 3-day Workshop for Trainers?

What you'll get:

- ❑ A chance to experience three action-packed, rich and multi-sensory days of accelerated learning for yourself
- ❑ A treasure trove of practical ideas you can apply immediately to your training
- ❑ A 150+ page, full colour manual – a complete resource to designing and delivering accelerated training
- ❑ The latest brain research and its implications for trainers and designers
- ❑ Personal coaching on your own course design
- ❑ Subscription to our free e-mail coaching tips for trainers
- ❑ Ongoing personal telephone and e-mail coaching on training design
- ❑ "Extra treat" workshops with renowned experts on Cartooning, Punch, Power and Presence and the Power of Storytelling

"Kaizen is to learning what Dyson is to vacuum cleaners!"

"More transferable than any other course I've ever been on"

"I've been training and consulting for 15 years - and believed there wasn't much more I could learn. I was wrong. This workshop challenged me to think about what I'm doing in a fundamental and powerful way"

"As a training novice, I came away with loads of ideas and new skills - and perhaps as important - ten times the confidence I had before"

"If you're a trainer, facilitator or coach, probably the most useful course you will ever attend"

"This stuff is so comprehensively far ahead of anything else I have experienced in the learning sphere, it is difficult to express how far it has moved me on. Kaizen's encyclopaedic knowledge of their stuff is truly impressive"

Visit our website on **www.kaizen-training.com** or call 01923 262278, or send an e-mail to **directors@kaizen-training.com** to find out the dates of our next workshop!

Substantial discounts offered to SEAL members!

Jenny Mosley and her team have great pleasure in announcing...

Whole School Training Days

You can invite and involve all your teachers, midday supervisors, classroom assistants and share in a vision of a happy school!

Our team can run these as Closure Days or they can work in your school during an ordinary day.

Cover your costs by hosting the day and inviting other delegates who pay their fees directly to you. Not only does the training reinvigorate everyone it helps team building.

The Arts Through Circle Time

We are thrilled to be able to offer you our latest range of training workshops;

* Power of Puppets
* The Wonder of Story Telling
* Splish Splash Splosh
* Drama
* Rhymes, Rhythms and Rounds

These can all be adapted to either Early Years, Primary or Secondary sectors of education.

Accredited Train The Trainer Courses for Primary & Secondary Teachers

Become formally accredited by Jenny in her model of Quality Circle Time and confident enough to teach other teachers how to use the model to realise the aims of PHSE, Citizenship, Self Esteem and Positive Behaviour.

New Catalogue

Bursting with old favourites and exciting newcomers the catalogue highlights resources to support early years, peaceful playtimes and the creation of dynamic, positive schools.

Conferences

We can contribute to conferences or help to structure one for you.

We can offer a range of powerful keynote speakers and fascinating workshops.

jenny mosley consultancies
releasing excellence through building self-esteem

28a Gloucester Road
Trowbridge
Wiltshire BA14 0AA
Tel: 01225 767157
Fax: 01225 755631

Website: www.circle-time.co.uk
Email: circletime@jennymosley.demon.co.uk

All our claims can be validated and we're happy to put you in touch with past clients.

For More Information, Call: 01225 767157